# visual
# creativity

# visual creativity

## Inspirational Ideas for Advertising, Animation and Digital Design

mario pricken

with 817 illustrations, 794 in colour

Thames & Hudson

# Contents

# Designer's Foreword

by Christine Klell

'Learning through play' could be the motto for this book. Its aim is to guide you into new spheres of creativity, and with its clearly structured content and innovative ideas, it will enable you to adopt all its methods in your own individual way. You can begin wherever you like, you can follow your instincts or read everything in the right order, but in any case, you will keep finding new paths to inspiration. Because the best training is the kind you do yourself, we have packed into this book everything we know about knowledge, and we give you a practical insight into how you can best learn to learn! Throughout the book you will find a whole range of exercises which you will almost always be able to do yourself because the most important tool that you need is right there at your disposal – namely, your head. I believe that there are two obvious signs that will show whether the book has achieved its full effect: firstly, if in the shortest possible time it starts showing signs of wear and tear; secondly, if you keep having to hunt for it because one of your colleagues has borrowed it yet again. If they do, that's not a problem, because we've designed it to be used as a practical handbook, not a decoration for your bookshelf. It's vital for me that form and content should go together, because this is all about creativity, and if you want to pass on knowledge of this sort of subject, why not try out new and creative ways of presenting that knowledge? Let the book take you into new fields. And if you feel like giving me some feedback, or expressing some ideas of your own, then I'd be delighted to hear from you at *info@christine-klell.com*

'You can begin wherever you like, you can follow your instincts or read everything in the right order, but in any case, you will keep finding new paths to inspiration.'

# Author's Foreword

by Mario Pricken

'Dream with your eyes open, and see with your eyes closed.'

For creatives working in fields such as advertising, film, photography, computer game development or animation, conditions are changing at a frightening speed: ideas are judged by international standards, technologies are evolving faster than you can master them, budgets are shrinking, and project deadlines are becoming tighter and tighter yet continue to demand longer and longer lists of new ideas. The only thing that hasn't changed is the way that ideas are developed: by instinct, from creatively gifted minds. Under these circumstances it's no surprise that even hardened professionals can sometimes get the feeling that they've reached the absolute limit of their creative powers. So, in this book I have tried to come up with methods that can be used by anyone who is open enough to want to extend and redefine those limits, for anyone who wants to create fascinating visual worlds and realize ideas that have never been seen before.

In the pages that follow, you'll find lots of new techniques and plenty of exercises that will help you to explore the ways in which internal and external worlds can interact, and intuitive visual strategies can be applied in a conscious, practical way. The guiding principle is: Dream with your eyes open, and see with your eyes closed. I will be taking you along new paths, so that the essence of creativity will become easier to grasp, and I will also be tapping into the resources of some of today's top creative minds. Read the interviews with these stars of the business, and you'll get a privileged insight into the sources and techniques that these exceptional talents draw upon. Many of them are speaking for the first time about their own visual worlds and the ways in which they develop the contents of their imaginations into new and striking ideas.

All the exercises and methods are illustrated with excellent examples of creative work from some of the most innovative studios all over the world, many of which are award-winners. My aim is not just to pass on my own experiences of working with top creative teams, but also to convey to you some of the sheer fun that I have had with them as a creative and an ideas man during our joint efforts to blaze new trails. To begin developing your creative skills as effectively as possible, you are encouraged to log on to my website: *www.idea-engineering.com*

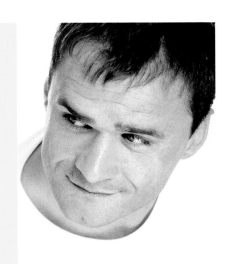

introduction

# 1.  Who Is This Book Aimed At?

**TEN-SECOND SUMMARY**   This book is for professionals in all creative fields, and it invites you to find out step by step what your creativity can achieve. It does not offer you theories, but provides concrete instructions and exercises to improve your powers of imagination, your visual range, and the practical ways in which your talent can be put to use.

This entire book revolves around creativity for creative thinkers. If you work in a field such as advertising, the media, the cinema, computer animation, game development, photography or illustration, you are bound to find plenty of ideas here to recharge your creative batteries, or to give them a jump-start. Anyone who works in these fields full-time needs to rise above daily routines, restrictive conditions, limited budgets and the usual constraints of time, to keep their enthusiasm going and their standards high.

The techniques are, however, just as exciting for students and for beginners, because they offer insights into the strategies of experts in the field, so that everyone can extend their own imaginative range as well as trying out new tools. So this book can be used by anyone who is searching for new visual worlds, and wants to send their imagination soaring to new heights.

Finally, however, this book is also directed at those who manage creative teams and guide the creative process. It's only through understanding the modes and structures of this process that the potential of those who are engaged in it can really be

fulfilled. As many of us have experienced for ourselves, a lack of this kind of understanding has led to ideas being treated as a kind of industrial product that must be churned out along the most rational lines possible. The consequence of this attitude is demotivation and frustration within the team, causing an unbridgeable gap between practical and budgetary constraints on the one side, and creative ideas and ideals on the other.

This book is intended for creatives in the following fields:

- advertising and marketing
- post-production and computer animation
- game design and development
- graphic art and design
- film and video
- photography
- electronic media
- cartoons and stop-motion animation
- new media
- industrial design
- virtual reality development
- architecture
- management of creative departments

## 2.   Getting The Most From This Book

### Experience the thrill of skydiving

If you want to read this book straight through like a novel, you're sure to get a lot of fun out of it. If, however, you want to learn something useful that you can use every day at work, then that method probably won't help you a lot. Experience suggests that it wouldn't be much use, for instance, to give you a graphic, detailed account of the thrill you get from skydiving if you've never actually done it. That kind of excitement can't be communicated – you have to feel it for yourself. Nobody knows this better than parents, who can try any number of times to advise their children which path to take, but know perfectly well that the advice will not be followed and the kids will go their own way.

One potential solution to the problem of the incommunicability of experience was proposed by the British philosopher and logician George Spencer Brown, who suggested the use of 'injunctive language'. This is language that does not attempt to explain, that does not formulate theories or convey knowledge; instead, by giving instructions, it leads to direct experience, which is of course the best way of learning. In practical terms, this means that you should sign up for a course in parachute jumping, learn how to pack your parachute, get into a plane, and then find out for yourself how wind, noise, temperature, and the unforgettable jump towards the earth can all combine to give you the thrill of skydiving. You can follow the same principle to extract the maximum of new creative skills from this book. Here you will find a constant stream of instructions that invite you to try out new ideas that will lead you to new creative adventures. I wonder whether you will choose to go for practical experience or the simple pleasures of reading.

### If it works, it must be right

The phenomenon of creativity is easier to observe than to define. Attempts to understand and explain it as an abstract ability have generally proved fruitless, and so it seems to me important that we should define it by way of its results rather than as a theory. Creativity, it could be said, becomes reality when it succeeds in giving visible, audible or tangible form to an imaginary idea, so that others can perceive it in the outside world. This is the process followed by the methods and exercises that are set out here. Whether other people's theories apply or not is irrelevant. What is far more important is the fact that some of these methods are highly effective, have led to fascinating results in the past, and in many cases have been used – either consciously or unconsciously – by generations of creative people. If it works, it must be right.

The good sense behind this idea can be shown by the following example taken from space travel: physics regards itself as an exact science, but its models and theories often make no claim to absolute truth; instead they seek to achieve a more or less functional, practical or conceptual simplicity. It was only by using this approach that NASA was able in the 1960s to carry out the extraordinarily complex project of landing a man on the moon. Today, of course, we recognize that our world picture is heliocentric; it is the sun and not the Earth that lies at the centre of our planetary system. Astonishingly, however, NASA's starting point for its first flights to the moon was a geocentric world picture – in other words, its basic premise was wrong. What is fascinating is the fact that despite the scientific falsity of the premise, it permitted a set of calculations that were precise enough to organize a successful project. It enabled

'I wonder whether you will choose to go for practical experience or the simple pleasures of reading.'

NASA to predict the time of arrival and to work out a detailed and safe landing area on the moon. The reason for this procedure was simple: if the model for the flightpath and landing had been based on a heliocentric world view, the mathematical technology available at the time would not have been able to cope. If it works, it must be right. So have a go at these methods and exercises, and find out for yourself whether they are 'right' or not. You will also discover ways in which you can put them to practical use on a day-to-day basis.

## Why so many illustrations?

I have chosen all these illustrations from the worlds of advertising, cinema, computer animation, games and music videos because they are all excellent examples of visual creativity. They are meant to illustrate ways of developing new ideas and exciting new concepts that will extend the range of your visual language. But under no circumstances should they be regarded as models for imitation or, even worse, plagiarism! The broad selection of materials, styles, media and concepts is intended to be a source of inspiration that will transport you beyond the boundaries of your own field and into other spheres of creative activity. For instance, you can combine photography with illustration, or game design with styles and ideas taken from music videos.

The basic idea is that you should enhance your visual creativity in order to come up with innovative and useful visions of your own. This will also lead to many different cultural elements and tastes blending together in a kind of global pictorial language, and I would like to think that my book will perhaps also contribute to a merging of media, styles, and other areas of creative activity.

## What can you expect from these methods?

If you use this as a handbook, and are interested in trying out new things in order to expand your range of choice and to gain more flexibility in your search for ideas, it will give you a lot of pleasure. Its main aim is to promote three vital areas of creative work, and to offer new methods that will extend the strategies that are pertinent to these areas.

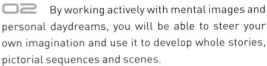 By enhancing your imaginative skills and improving your ability to consciously shape and exploit the power of visual imagery, you will open the door into exciting new territories.

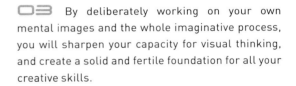 By working actively with mental images and personal daydreams, you will be able to steer your own imagination and use it to develop whole stories, pictorial sequences and scenes.

By deliberately working on your own mental images and the whole imaginative process, you will sharpen your capacity for visual thinking, and create a solid and fertile foundation for all your creative skills.

part 01

**Visual Evolution**

part 01

# 1.  The Frontiers Of Your Imagination

**TEN-SECOND SUMMARY**   Modern technology has given limitless freedom to the creative mind. We no longer ask how far we can go with our ideas, but how far we want to go. Many people forget, however, that stories, ideas and punchlines are the things that give pictures the ability to attract people's attention.

In one of his major works, the Austrian-born philosopher Ludwig Wittgenstein claimed that the frontiers of our language were also the frontiers of our world. In certain respects, this concept can also be applied to the inner world of the creative imagination. The frontiers of our imaginations are the frontiers of our world. This seems all the more plausible when you take into account the fact that today everything that springs from the imagination can be experienced as virtual reality through computer technology. Suddenly the question is no longer how far you can go with a new idea, but how far you want to go. The magic formula for advertising, films, computer animation and photography now reads 'Everything is possible'. There is indeed a kind of magic in the way that we can create totally new worlds, or expand and transform existing ones. We can even shift events in time and space, and bring the past back into the present. We can be passive spectators, or we can take part in the action. Computer games, for instance, allow us to transcend our own physical limitations, and to take on any role we wish; we can be ourselves, or we can be anyone else we choose to be.

The interchange between computer, film, TV, games, the Internet and mobile phones enables us to move freely out of this world and into the world of the imagination. The World Wide Web, DVDs, satellite TV and the information super-highway all provide us with the hardware to create a vast network of images that cross cultural boundaries and can encompass the entire globe. However, despite the euphoria of this technological wizardry and its unlimited potential, we must never lose sight of one crucial fact: all these technologies and their owners require a ceaseless flow of new content, original ideas, entertaining stories that will provide excitement, surprise and delight. The fuel that drives these engines is and will always be creativity. The challenge confronting the creative minds of today is to keep pushing back the frontiers of the imagination, to create new things and

to think what was previously unthinkable. We need ideas, we need fantasy to open up new territories and to create dramatic, aesthetic, sensory illusions that are different from those that we are used to. Creatives are now subjected to greater pressures than ever, and are becoming more and more aware that they are approaching the limits of their intuitive skills. They are therefore looking for new ways, new sources of inspiration to help them develop ideas that will stand up to the increasingly fierce demands of today's international market.

You will find this kind of inspiration in the chapters that follow, and the methods they describe will make you more aware of how you yourself can work more creatively, and of how you can even give your instincts a kick-start on their way to the promised land of the Big Idea.

## Creativity is more important than technology

Attention is the goal of our media-based society. Successful creatives are those that know how to attract attention and use their images to reach the hearts and minds of the group they are targeting. This is true for advertising, the cinema, and all other media – they all share the aim of communicating messages and stories. John Lasseter, whose 1990s film *Toy Story* brought animated stories to life, once made the following apposite remark: 'We're storytellers who happen to use computers. Story and characters come first and that is what drives everything we do. It's not about technology or computer tricks; it's about teaching people to be surprised again.'

It's much the same with advertising, for here too the aim must be to stir the emotions, to surprise and astonish. With the massive expansion of information technology, the quest for unmistakable trademarks and logos has become increasingly desperate. An established corporate design is often no longer enough to achieve recognition, and instead what is required is a brand image, a distinct and unique picture that will leave no room for confusion. An image that is not underpinned by an idea, that does not follow a precise direction or does not contain a definite message, is a worthless image of no intrinsic value – a beautiful package with nothing inside.

Every day we can see for ourselves that stories, ideas and punchlines endow images with a certain indefinable energy which magnetically draws our attention to them. It is therefore all the more surprising that specialist journals, conferences and university courses devote far more attention to the subject of technology than to that of creativity. Perhaps the reason is that the whole process of invention is still perceived as some kind of magician's cabinet, inside which lies a completely mysterious working mechanism that is best left alone. 'Either you're creative or you're not' is a comment I keep

hearing. And after talking with a number of international stars of the field, I soon came to realize where this idea has sprung from. Despite their success, very few of them genuinely understand what it is that drives them onward in their quest for new ideas. In other words, most of them are unable to explain their creativity, because they do what they do by instinct alone.

This is precisely the point at which it seems to me that things get exciting. What really interests me is those invisible processes that take place deep down in the human mind to fashion creative ideas. Together with different teams and in different contexts according to the needs of the moment, I have developed some useful practical methods, and I believe these will be of particular benefit to professionals who are willing to experiment in their search for new directions.

## 2.   Inside A Creative Mind

**TEN-SECOND SUMMARY**   Even if we seldom realize it, 40 per cent of our waking hours are spent among imaginary pictures. Top creatives distinguish themselves from the rest by their conscious use of this source, developing extraordinary images through their inspired fantasies. But however individual their ideas may be, these also depend on the individuality of the methods they use to produce and exploit the inner flood of images.

As a creative, you are engaged on a daily adventure, smuggling new ideas into the world. You are able to do this mainly because you can see things that do not exist. Many people call this power imagination or fantasy, but others call it daydreaming or visual thinking. What do these terms signify? A glance at the dictionary will tell you that 'imagination' is derived from the Latin word *imago*, which means 'likeness'. For the Romans the term *imaginatio* also meant the active power of pictures, or active vision. The word 'fantasy' has the same meaning, but is derived from the Greek *phantasma*. The etymology, however, is of little help to us nowadays, for over the last few centuries these concepts have been used in many different ways. The fact that we can no longer define them with any clarity is probably due also to their being regarded by many levels of society as inferior forms of mental activity. This is quite extraordinary when one considers that according to Dr Eric Klinger, a pioneer in the study of daydreams, we spend some 40 per cent of our time wandering through these inner worlds. Fantasy, imagination, daydreams – these are so normal and so universal that most people are not even conscious of the pleasure they are treating themselves to, day by day. Just as fish don't know they're getting wet, human beings don't know they're being constantly flooded by a sea of imaginary pictures.

Sometimes we indulge in images of the past, calling up our memories, but the next moment we can be planning for something in the future. Jerome Singer, a leading expert on this subject, says that daydreams are distinguished by the fact that they take our attention away from perceiving the real world outside, and direct it to the charms of the inner world.

Thus they can transport us to places thousands of miles away. We can visit an old friend, we can tell the boss precisely what we think of him, we can travel through space and time, and we can switch effortlessly from one scene or situation to another. The imagination enables us to enter different worlds and realities without being physically present in them. It is this potential that makes daydreams the perfect vehicle for developing new, creative ideas. These allow us to make trial runs without the slightest risk – we can act out any scenario, and absolutely nothing can go wrong.

If in the next few days you should find yourself using public transport, take the opportunity to do a little research: have a look at other people daydreaming. Just let your eyes wander over the rows of seats, and you can be quite sure that there will be just as many passengers gazing into space as passengers concentrating on their book or newspaper. They're wide awake, but their eyes appear to see nothing. Only their expression reveals from time to time that something is happening inside – from little movements of the lips right through to major transformations, you can see that they're visualizing something or someone inside their daydreams. When creative people are searching for new ideas, they use exactly the same source. The difference is that they are usually conscious of these images, and may even actively guide them towards a particular end. They might, for instance, try to picture something, and then combine it with another piece of work taken from their memory, adding new scenes, playing with new perspectives, outlining impossible scenarios or inventing creatures that no one else could possibly envisage.

## The essence of the imagination

Visual thinking is a particularly well-developed faculty in most people that are professionally involved in advertising, film, 3D animation and game development. But as has already been pointed out, the individuality of their ideas is matched by the individuality of their methods, those internal processes of image production. Many would describe the images in their mind's eye as clear and vivid, almost as if they could see them physically in the real world. Others, however, have only a vague idea, and would certainly not talk of 'seeing' their images with any degree of clarity. Their pictures do not appear three-dimensional, are often colourless, or are perceived as if through a kind of mist. The list of descriptions is potentially endless, and so it makes sense to jettison the assumption that the images and daydreams of creatives are always clear and colourful and solid, like films and photos. Studies have shown that only about five per cent of people have eidetic vision, meaning that they can see things with total, three-dimensional clarity.

In order to illustrate what I'm getting at here, I'd like to invite you to play a little game which will demonstrate just how common and present our inner images are, and how in all their forms they are able to produce a tangible effect. Give yourself a moment or two, and imagine taking a ripe lemon in your hand and cutting it right through the middle with a knife. You can see the juicy yellow flesh and you can smell that typical lemony tang. Now imagine running your tongue over the moist flesh, and then biting into it. In most people, this imagined action will lead to intense physiological reactions: there will be a strong flow of saliva, a little shudder, or even – as tests have shown –

the release of enzymes. It doesn't actually matter much how vividly you see the lemon. The fascinating thing is that the imaginary picture can evidently stimulate the body in exactly the same way as biting into a real lemon.

Another equally interesting aspect of this process is the fact that whatever information or stimulus we absorb through our senses of sight, touch, hearing, taste or smell can also set in motion the mental processes of the imagination. You might hear someone call your name, and even before you turn round, you have a mental image of the person whose voice you have recognized. You might open a bottle of perfume that you haven't used for ages, and the scent that greets you will immediately transport you back to the good old days, although you were not even thinking of them and had certainly not made any conscious decision to do so. You may have had similar experiences when reading a particularly exciting book. In a few very rare cases, people are aware of individual letters, but most of us take in the words. In fact, though, it is not simply the words that we see, for in reading we also formulate meaning and this comes to us in the form of images. We set one image next to another, and in this way we link the threads of the story into a pattern. A gripping novel will let your imagination fly, and its scenes will run before your mind's eye just like a film. For many people, reading a book is like having a cinema in their heads. It's often interesting to see how people react when they see the film of a novel they have read. They enter the cinema with eager anticipation, but a couple of hours later they come out again with frowns of disappointment. Evidently the director and his crew had very different images in their minds from those of the film-goer.

'A gripping novel will let your imagination fly, and its scenes will run before your mind's eye just like a film. For many people, reading a book is like having a cinema in their heads.'

This is perhaps the classic example of how one and the same stimulus can arouse totally different images in different people. This does not, of course, tell us whose image was right or even better – that of the director or that of the film-goer. All one can say is that the director was able to make a personal image visible to others.

Of course, imaginary pictures can also come into being independently of the outside world and of our senses. You need only think of instinctive needs such as hunger or sexual desire. It may be that hunger will produce, for instance, an imaginary pizza, and what is astonishing about this is that your visual fantasy will almost always be accompanied by a multisensory experience. You can smell the pizza, its taste makes your mouth water, and you can even feel the warm crisp pastry in your fingers as you pick it up. Many mental images are based on our memories and past experiences, and it is these that provide the raw material for our imaginings.

An equally effective spur is emotions such as fear, hope or anger. Most common of all is the nightly flow of images that come to us in our dreams, and these may include the dreams we have before we sleep, in which we can consciously manipulate scenes and deliberately steer real-life situations to imagined endings. The complexity of these mental processes has been clearly demonstrated by modern research, such as that carried out by the neurologist Oliver Sachs: 'We know today that in the human brain there are fifty different visual centres, all of which work independently and autonomously. They are all connected with different aspects of the visual world: with colour, movement, impressions of space, angles, forms, contrast and many more.' And yet he is convinced that ultimately there is no screen on which all these impressions can be projected together so that they can be viewed by you, the observer. What apparently happens is that there is a constant dialogue between these fifty brain centres. You might imagine this interaction in terms of an orchestra, with every centre playing an individual instrument, but all of these combining together in a single harmony, composing and playing the music of our reality and our imagination.

## Is there such a thing as inner blindness?

There are people who find it almost impossible to form mental images or to think visually. One must, however, avoid the premature assumption that they are less creative than others or that they are in some way handicapped. On the contrary, many of them have simply developed a different inner world which is characterized by a greater emphasis on hearing, emotion, taste or smell. In *The Doors of Perception*, the writer Aldous Huxley gave a vivid description of what it is like to be completely devoid of visual imagination: 'I am and, for as long as I can remember, I have always been a poor visualizer. Words, even the pregnant words of poets, do not evoke pictures in my mind. No hypnagogic visions greet me on the verge of sleep. When I recall something, the memory does not present itself to me as a vividly seen event or object. By an effort of the will, I can evoke a not very vivid image of what happened yesterday afternoon.... But such images have little substance and absolutely no autonomous life of their own. They stand to real, perceived objects in the same relation as Homer's ghosts stood to the

'It may be that hunger will produce, for instance, an imaginary pizza, and what is astonishing about this is that your visual fantasy will almost always be accompanied by a multisensory experience.'

men of flesh and blood, who came to visit them in the shades. Only when I have a high temperature do my mental images come to independent life. To those in whom the faculty of visualization is strong my inner world must seem curiously drab, limited and uninteresting.'

There are many similar but highly gifted people in the fields of music, literature and even copywriting.

They are no less creative, but their creativity manifests itself in different ways from that of the visually gifted. Nevertheless, those whose visual imagination is underdeveloped can, with practice, build it up and improve it step by step. So long as it gives pleasure, there is no reason why anyone should not be able to expand and enrich his or her own creative abilities and inner, imaginative world.

'Those whose visual imagination is underdeveloped can, with practice, build it up and improve it step by step.'

# 3.   Inside The Imaginations Of Top Creatives

**TEN-SECOND SUMMARY**   Thirteen illuminating interviews with top international creatives give you insight into their visual thinking and their ways of dealing with the inner world of the imagination. It is clear that creativity is not a box of tricks. If you read these interviews closely, you will get to know some successful creative strategies, and you will see that there is a close connection between an instinctive talent and the conscious processing of inner images.

On the pages that follow you will find extracts from interviews with top creatives including Ben Snow of ILM, the director Daniel Kleinman, and Tracy Wong, the mastermind behind the American ad agency Wongdoody. The text has been selected to give you revealing insights into the inner worlds of these outstanding talents. As well as these interviews, I have had countless conversations with many experts in the fields of advertising, computer animation, film and game development, and these have convinced me beyond doubt that visual thinking plays a central role in creativity. The ability to imagine pictures is inseparably bound up with one's sense of fantasy, and daydreams are often used as a kind of platform from which to launch new and innovative ideas. The development of original visual worlds, which redefine the frontiers of our pictorial language, is largely dependent on this faculty.

And yet despite the virtual unanimity and the confirmation offered by scientific research, there remains a certain dissatisfaction, and a large number of new questions keep springing to mind. What, for instance, do these imaginary worlds that enable us to develop our creativity actually look like? What exactly is it that gives creatives their special ability to come up with one original idea after another so quickly? How do they set about adding the details to their initial idea? To these fascinating questions some of our experts give concrete and illuminating answers, while others simply shrug their shoulders because they experience their creativity as an ongoing and mainly automatic process. The interviews will give you an idea of the different levels and degrees of sharpness with which this process unfolds. Some people, for instance, can describe what their inner images look like, but they have no idea how they manipulate or mould them in order to obtain the desired results. Perhaps they have never thought about whether or not the pictures move, or how concretely they must visualize them in order to modify, combine or split them. And why should they do so, since their intuition has probably been enough to achieve their excellent results? Perhaps they have never had any real need or incentive to expand their talents through a conscious exposure to new methods.

I think that one of the most important aspects of these interviews is that they clearly demonstrate that creativity is not a magic trick. The claim that 'either you're creative or you're not' simply means that the speaker has no idea what he is doing in order to achieve his results, but is acting purely on instinct. Anyone with a degree of curiosity, who is willing to experiment in order to expand his or her range of creative strategies, will derive a great deal of pleasure from the exercises in Part 2, for a certain amount of awareness about your own creative processes is essential if you want to add new tools to the existing kit. Only those who know how their own creativity functions will be able deliberately to adopt and adapt the strategies of others, to experiment with them, and to find suitable means of using them in the future.

The aim of all the exercises in this book is to give you more freedom and flexibility to decide how you want to expand your gifts, and whether you want to make use of some new tools in order to turn your weaknesses into strengths.

## 3.1 Creative Director

Tracy Wong is Creative Director and Chairman of the ad agency Wongdoody. He has won over 300 awards and is considered to be one of the top fifty creatives worldwide. Peter Liguori, President of FX Network, said of him: 'Every ten or fifteen years, advertising produces some really extraordinary person and, infrequently, that person comes up from the art direction side of the business, someone who thinks with his or her eyes.'

① **Mario:** Tracy, as a Creative Director, you're constantly on the lookout for new visual ideas and picture worlds. What, in your opinion, is the connection between serious creative talent and the inner world of imagination and fantasy?

**Tracy:** Creative talent comes from within. It comes from your personal world of imagination, fantasy, whatever you want to call it. There is no separation. Creativity allows you to see beyond what the world sees right now, what is known, what already exists. In high school and college, I was very much into math – advanced calculus, differentials, engineering stuff. It struck me back then how much creativity played a part in solving what I thought were hard, completely logical problems. On a very, very simplistic level, I can understand where Einstein was coming from. It's the ability to envision things that aren't there that takes us to new places. That's the creative process. That's the imagination at work. It applies to everything in life. Cooking. Kicking a soccer ball. Physics. Selling something.

② **Mario:** Creatives describe the intensity and clarity of their mental images in a wide variety of ways. Many see their ideas as clearly in front of them as if they were real. Others describe these images as vague notions or unreal-seeming picture compositions. How would you describe the pictures created by your imagination and your mental picture worlds?

**Tracy:** Sometimes the images I see when trying to solve a creative problem are crystal clear. They come in an instant. Sometimes the images are blurred. Sometimes the images never come at all and I have to work at finding them. I think truly gifted artists have clear images all of the time. I've heard Mozart felt like he was just channelling from another place. The notes just came rushing into his head and down into his hands right onto paper. I've heard Stephen King say pretty much the same thing as he sits down to write. But most of us aren't so blessed. On seldom occasions, when I've finished an assignment, it's exactly as I had envisioned it from the very start. But most of the time, inspiration doesn't quite fit our tight deadlines and vision has to be replaced by plain toil and sweat. If I could understand or explain when or where these creative visions come from, I would have retired to my very own island by now.

③ **Mario:** What role do daydreams and the world of the imagination play in the life of a creative person?

**Tracy:** Daydreaming and allowing your imagination to wander are essential to a creative person. That's what we do for a living. We wander, dream, search, fantasize, fart around – whatever you want to call it – until we find an answer. Mind you, we have to do that within the constraints of the business world, which is full of things that aren't conducive to daydreaming, a world full of deadlines, bureaucracy, politics, finances and other restrictions.

④ **Mario:** What, in your opinion, gives pictures the power to arouse certain feelings in people?

**Tracy:** Pictures are the quickest, clearest and most succinct way to communicate on a human level. What we see with our eyes goes straight to our hearts. Visuals trigger feelings the quickest, go the deepest and stay with us the longest. This is true for anyone on the planet, no matter what their race, creed, culture, sex or age. Words can't do that.

## 3.2 Visual Effects Supervisor

interview

(FRANK PETZOLD)

Frank Petzold began his career as a freelance cameraman and visual effects operator. Since 1994 he has worked at Tippett Studio in California, where he has worked as Visual Effects Supervisor on films that include The Ring, Evolution, Hollow Man, The Haunting, Starship Troopers and Armageddon. He was nominated for an Oscar for his work on Hollow Man.

① **Mario:** Aside from all the specialist knowledge that you bring to your job, I'm interested to know what inspires you when you're looking for ideas.

**Frank:** I think it's important to have a desk that looks messy, rather like a fourteen-year-old's bedroom. I have loads of stuff lying around that I often haven't tidied up for months, and sometimes an idea will just emerge. I need it like that; creativity works best that way for me. I get the same sort of permanent stimulation from our open-plan office. I also keep going back to references like cartoons and models by Tex Avery and Ray Harryhausen. These are the kind of references you just have in your head and you use to lead to you to something new and inspiring.

② **Mario:** Your job is to look for new visual ideas every day. What really inspires you? What stimulates your imagination?

**Frank:** I set aside two days a week when I don't do anything else other than think about things, playing with ideas or working on concepts together with other creatives. For example, we might start with the task of getting across to the viewer that a character is blind but that he can see in a strange way, perhaps with telepathy or something like that. Sometimes I might then go into the studio to experiment; for instance, I might shake up some aluminium powder in a container that's been lit from behind, and let myself be inspired by the visual effects it creates. Or you can try doing something you did as a child. You can look in the mirror and see the picture start to twist and become distorted.

③ **Mario:** Many creatives describe the intensity and clarity of their inner ideas in vastly different ways. How would you describe your ideas, or the pictures that you see in front of your inner eye?

**Frank:** I start with an inner dialogue. I try to form my own outline of an object or a creature in thought-pictures. That way, I can slowly build up a more detailed picture in my head. Occasionally I just begin with a simple animation of a creature in wire form. Quite automatically a clear picture starts to form, and sometimes a whole story that explains the character visually and physically. It's really important for me to learn as much about my 'project' as possible. In a team we then try to work out what characteristics will be needed in order to truly bring the character to life.

④ **Mario:** How do you use your imagination to work on new ideas or play through scenes in your head?

**Frank:** A monster as tall as a house needs a greater build-up of tension than a tiny fly would. The more often I run through the sequence in my head, the better the 'cut' that I see in my inner eye. My inner dialogue also plays a big part in getting the timing of the film right. This kind of advance planning is needed for visual effects that require a great deal of work, so that the different tasks can later be divided up within the team. When the time comes to begin production, the end product has already been complete in my head for a long time.

## 3.3  Graphic Designer

Jennifer Sterling is the founder of Sterling Design in San Francisco, a studio that was chosen as one of the top twelve worldwide by Graphis Design Annual. She has won countless awards for her graphic design and her work has been included in museum collections all over Europe and America. She is a true innovator whose projects are regularly chosen to appear in design books and annuals.

① Mario: Do you think there's a connection between internal pictures and creative aptitude? How do you use your imagination and fantasy when you need to develop ideas?

Jennifer: It depends on how you measure creative aptitude. I think there's a connection between internal pictures and originality. Too often designers (this term I use lightly) do what I call 'the Christopher Columbus discovery of America' approach to design. (There were people in America before he arrived, we call them Native Americans.) For instance you wouldn't walk out to your car and upon finding a stranger sitting in it have them exclaim that they had 'discovered' it. Many designers do just that. They discover it on page 183 of *Communication Arts* magazine. I'm sure how to answer the second question, in that my imagination doesn't turn off. This isn't the benefit you may think as it leads me to imagine that the phone company won't turn off my phone if I procrastinate or that maybe I don't even really need a phone or that I should move to a remote place that doesn't have phones or that....see?

② Mario: Many creatives know only very little about how they develop good ideas. And this comes as no great surprise, as it's often the case that the things we're best at are the things we do subconsciously. How does this work with you, do you have an understanding of how you develop your ideas and of the inner procedures you go through in order to achieve them?

Jennifer: At times I'll actually dream layouts and ideas. I'm so used to this, I managed to wake myself and record these. Usually my subconscious will continue to explore an idea or design while I'm

putting down the meat and potatoes of the concept. I start in the same manner each time. I meet with the client and every person on the client end who has a hand in the decision-making. It doesn't do the client any good to put a low-level person in place to answer high-level corporate decisions regarding the company's message. It's not that they aren't qualified to handle producing the collateral in question; it's that they might not have the answers to the high-level data that needs to be asked and answered to deliver that particular piece of collateral. By delving down into what is innovative to them you let them define their image. The concept always creates the form. I never discuss the design until this concept platform stage is completed. It's never a surprise then that the annual report ends up large and red. If you have to defend the concept, you'll have to defend the design.

③ Mario: At what time are you able to daydream most successfully and what particularly fires your imagination?

Jennifer: I hate to say it, but while driving. I'm probably a menace on the road as huge stretches of my commute along the Golden Gate Bridge don't even register as I'm playing internally with layouts.

④ Mario: When a good idea suddenly pops up or an unusual scene or picture occurs to you, how do you then record your ideas so that you don't forget them or lose some of the detail?

Jennifer: Actually I bought a mini recorder, particularly for in the car but I kept erasing or recording over the data, so now I just call my phone and leave myself a message.

## 3.4  Director

Daniel Kleinman is an internationally renowned director of ads and music videos. His work for clients including Audi, DaimlerChrysler, Microsoft and General Motors has won multiple awards, and his work in the music industry includes videos for Madonna, Fleetwood Mac and Simple Minds. He has also brought his individual visual stamp to the title sequences of the last four James Bond movies.

① **Mario:** Daniel, advertising has an insatiable appetite for new and exciting picture worlds. From where do you get the ideas and inspiration that allow you to continually develop new visual worlds?

**Daniel:** I keep an open mind and pay attention to varied visual sources; these could be magazines, film, painting, museums, galleries, photography, theatre and of course lots of TV. I also drink.

② **Mario:** A lot of top creatives were prolific daydreamers as children, which is why they often had problems at home or school. What role did daydreams play during your childhood?

**Daniel:** I was thought of as a bit of a daydreamer at school, partly because I found school and most of the teachers boring. The ability to teach in a stimulating way, encouraging students to want to learn more, is a gift. Not many of my teachers had it; luckily for me, my parents did. I probably did daydream a lot, and not being good at or interested in sport at all, spent all my spare time drawing fantasy scientific worlds with my best friend, who due to illness, not inclination, was forced to explore the internal rather than external world.

③ **Mario:** How has the way you use your imagination and the way you daydream changed since you were a child?

**Daniel:** I now charge people for it.

④ **Mario:** Many creatives describe the process of getting ideas as a game involving inner pictures and ideas. Picture elements are often combined, scenes changed and new material added. If you were to think now about how you personally develop ideas, how would you describe the process you go through?

**Daniel:** I either have an immediate vision of how I want something to be or it comes together slowly over a period of time. It can help not to think of the problem you are trying to solve and let your subconscious work on it. Memory is made up of many different parts and each time these disparate parts come together to form a memory, the memory is subtly different although you are not aware that it is. Creative thinking can work in a similar way, leave it, then each time you come back to it is a bit further on. I also think it important to be open-minded about the input of those around you. Probably the most important practical part of the process is drawing out thumbnail sketches.

⑤ **Mario:** Are you able to consciously control, summon up and influence your inner fantasy worlds and pictures?

**Daniel:** I like to draw out options and, if practical, leave as many open as possible, leaving decisions for the editing process. Even if one were able to play out scenes in one's head, the practicality of filming will mean they are different. One can of course have a sense of the best way of doing things, which I think comes more from experience than imagining every different possibility.

⑥ **Mario:** Can you reveal any kind of method or trick that you've used to turn mental pictures into ideas or to improve your imaginative powers?

**Daniel:** I advise everybody, whatever they do, to take up life-drawing, which hones one's ability to look, imagine and be decisive.

## 3.5 Motion Graphics

interview

(MATTHIAS ZENTNER)

Matthias Zentner is the founder of the Munich-based company Velvet, which has won over a hundred national and international awards for its work in commercials, broadcast design, and video and installation art. Today Matthias is one of the most creative minds in the field, who brings the same demand for perfection and constant innovation to his work in directing, editing, art direction and sound design.

① **Mario:** When you are looking for a new idea, what do you concentrate on most, the technical possibilities or your own creativity and imagination?

**Matthias:** I deliberately forget what is technically possible, and free myself from the constraints of technology. I try not to put limits on my imagination. It's during the next stage that technology starts to be important, when I ask myself what I need to make a great idea into a flawless piece of work.

② **Mario:** What do your mental images look like, for instance when you're working on a TV commercial or a title design?

**Matthias:** Ideas for TV ads usually come into my head as complete films. There's no mental block or anything like that. I have no idea where they come from. Perhaps it's a matter of training; over the years, you just learn to come up with ideas to meet tight deadlines. If I'm scouting for locations, for instance, I picture the finished film taking place there. In that way I get a feeling for whether it works, if the light is right, the angle, the mood, all those things. It often happens that I visualize things in this way and these images sometimes act as a trigger for new and different ideas. It's a sort of stream of consciousness inside me that I can use to run through scenes and work on ideas. It works like a domino effect: one idea appears and that one leads to the next image and the next one and so on in a chain reaction. This happens to me very frequently.

③ **Mario:** I know that your schedule is packed and that your day-to-day business leaves no room for creative breaks. Do you still manage to find time to lose yourself in daydreams or fantasies?

**Matthias:** Oh yes, they are fixed and they're with me all the time in any case. Don't forget, my job means that I must always be ready and always on the search for ideas. My daydreams and imaginings recharge my motivation and energy levels and help to keep me pushing ahead. Sometimes it happens that I come unstuck with one of my own ideas. Perhaps something is missing, but I note it down and then forget about it. After a few months, the idea might crop up again and I'll take it further and do something with it. The way the subconscious works is amazing.

④ **Mario:** What special ways do you have of developing your ideas, when you are looking for an unusual visual solution?

**Matthias:** I write most of my ideas down. When I'm writing, it's like being in a sort of trance. Often I don't know exactly what I'm writing, and when it's finished, I can't remember what I wrote. When I'm doing it, I have a very clear image in my head, but I put it into words. It can sometimes happen that the writing doesn't flow properly and I'll realize that something isn't working. Writing breaks down my mental images into pieces, so I can find out if anything is missing and where another image or transition or adjustment might be needed. Writing works as a form of control for me: it tells me if everything is okay.

## 3.6 Photographer

Erwin Olaf's supreme skill and amazing visual creativity have created astonishing new visual worlds and put him among the ranks of the world's best photographers. His international commissions have come from brands including Microsoft, Nintendo, Nokia, Diesel and Virgin. His regular exhibitions and unconventional music videos have been published in eight illustrated books and have brought him many prestigious awards.

① Mario: When you search for ideas and you try to develop them, do they come to you as mental pictures? How would you describe them?

Erwin: It's a contour of a picture – it's not really a clear picture. For example, my new series of photos focuses on a mother–son relationship. It has turned out as eight pictures and a short movie. The boy is completely dressed in rubber and the mother as well. And I don't know why, but it is great material to photograph. The setting is a living room and house that is completely decorated with floral wallpaper – it is present in every picture. The starting idea for this shoot was a child in a decadent outfit in a room with floral wallpaper, which is divided by light. You have the light coming into the room and divide the room into a light and a dark part. That was how I wanted to play with the light. Somebody told me a story about working in a shop that sells fetish clothing and he said that someone called asking for a fetish outfit in a child's size and that gave me the idea. This story was told to me three or four years ago and now I'm working with it – so it's a vague outline and a basis for somewhere to start.

② Mario: So your imagination plays a very big role in your work?

Erwin: Yes. It's my goldmine. The older I get and the more experience I acquire, the richer that experience is. You can relate it to being a good sportsman: here it's not the muscles but the imagination that can be developed. I am often asked to fill in some of the gaps in the concepts of directors. Years ago it took me days or weeks to find ideas, but now I find ideas in a conversation. It is funny because you can obviously train your imagination as well.

③ Mario: What has improved? The visual imagination?

Erwin: Yes, the visual imagination, because you can actually paint these ideas in your own mind. I can close my eyes and there it is, I can see the atmosphere of how it is supposed to be in the picture. But I realize and visualize the details for the first time when I am on the set. This has to do with the consequences that my idea has. The financial and technical consequences of ideas. Because some people say that they have great ideas, but amazing ideas are everywhere. It is the way you catch them and get them in your camera. There are two things that have to work together – a fantastic idea and then how you bring it to life. There are two other things I really need. Eighty per cent of my work is imagination and then the two critical things that I need are a deadline and a budget. If I don't have these then I panic.

④ Mario: How intense and clear are your mental images?

Erwin: They are in colour and they are clear in the distance, but once I get closer to them and study them, they become unclear. I cannot control these pictures in the first instance. What I can do is once the picture comes up, then I can hold on to it. When I need to recall the picture, I can control it more. So I can work around it. The pure basic idea that you see, you cannot control, but then you start the process of questioning critically whether this is a good idea. That is not the same day, not the same period, the very same moment, but there are other opportunities when you are more relaxed and recall the image. Then you can control the image.

## 3.7 Video Game Designer

Chris Taylor has worked in the video game industry for over thirteen years and his many hit games have ranked him among the top fifty creatives in his field. In 1998 he founded Gas Powered Games in Seattle. The company's aim is to use innovative ideas to redefine the frontiers of conventional computer gaming.

① **Mario:** If you want to develop a spectacular new landscape, for example, to what extent do you take your cue from reality and to what extent do you simply go with your imagination?

**Chris:** I like to dream stuff up in my imagination and use that to guide the super-talented and creative people that I work with... they do the really hard work. They take my words and ideas and turn that into reality; 3D models, animation, textures and sound. I like to use popular concepts and established visual elements to create new things but with a familiar feeling that lives in it... leaving the player (of the computer game) with a sense that they understand it and it feels comfortable. This is probably the thing that I bring to the process more than anything else.

② **Mario:** Do you flick enthusiastically through magazines or watch films or are you someone who falls back on their own inner pictures and allows themselves to be led by their own imagination?

**Chris:** I would say that books and music are more of an influence in this respect. It's strange but I can play a song and visualize more than when I use visual aids... and to a somewhat similar extent, when I read books. The thing about music is that the imagery is built constructed emotionally instead of visually or mechanically. This is powerful because when I describe a concept or new idea, it has the emotional stuff baked right in.

③ **Mario:** A lot of top creatives were prolific daydreamers as children. What role did daydreams play during your childhood?

**Chris:** Oh boy, I was definitely a daydreamer. I am also a big night-time dreamer as well. My imagination has served me very well, but it's also capable of creating images that are powerful and somewhat disconcerting. It has taken me a long time to harness my imagination. And yes, I had my challenges in school, but luckily I was able to focus that into computer games which the school embraced and rewarded me for.

④ **Mario:** When you're working on ideas for a game, do you adapt your ideas in your mind's eye? Do you play around with your ideas or do you know right from the start what the end results will look like?

**Chris:** In the early stages I toss ideas around in my head. I use a system whereby if I forget an idea, I figure it wasn't that good. It's like a natural selection process. When the time is right I start talking about an idea, and that helps me to lubricate my imagination and fill in the details of my overall vision. Once I do that, I can start to write my ideas down and have people provide feedback. When working with visual ideas, the largest transformation comes when the ideas are made into concepts... because often, the concept can come out completely different than I had imagined it... which is fine with me because they often come out better.

⑤ **Mario:** Can you reveal any kind of method or trick that you've used to turn mental pictures into creative ideas or to improve your imaginative powers?

**Chris:** I am verbose, and I always have been. My thing is to work with people who are good listeners. When I first start talking, the idea is boring or lacks some essential spark. As I talk, the idea fills in, and I solve logistical challenges or mechanical problems with the idea while the words are coming out of my mouth. My advice for anyone who works creatively like this is to find the right team that matches the style they are most comfortable with. The creative sphincter will snap shut when the wrong people are involved in the process.

# 3.8  Visual Effects Supervisor

interview
(BEN SNOW)

Since 1994, Ben Snow has worked for the special effects company Industrial Light & Magic, founded by George Lucas. One of his first projects was producing 3D computer images for Star Trek. He has been nominated for an Academy Award and has produced fascinating new visualworlds as a visual effects supervisor for movies including Twister, Deep Impact, The Mummy and Star Wars Episode II: Attack of the Clones.

① **Mario:** Ben, your success is based to a large extent on fantastic visual ideas in which you constantly create new picture worlds. What, in your opinion, is the connection between serious creative talent and the inner world of imagination and fantasy?

**Ben:** Undoubtedly having a rich inner world of imagination and fantasy is helpful to people working creatively. The question makes me a little uncomfortable, because it reminds me how people's creativity is somehow judged by the way they come across in the 'outer' world, even by them. I was never any good at drawing, and, strangely in retrospect, I thought this would mean it would be hard to pursue a creative career, even though I'd always daydreamed and made up stories and fantasies as a kid, and enjoyed amateur film-making and photography. I trained in computing and film, and there was always a technical versus artistic friction in my life, even in my first few years working as an artist in television commercials and post-production. My technical background made me insecure about my creative side.

② **Mario:** Creatives describe the intensity and clarity of their mental images in a wide variety of ways. How would you describe the pictures created by your imagination and your mental picture worlds?

**Ben:** I definitely tend towards images as notions, or even as abstracted ideas. Often I'll almost be imagining it as a written idea, and actually find that writing the idea down helps me start thinking about what it will look like visually. This is handy for communicating ideas.

③ **Mario:** When you're working on an idea for a visual effects project, do you adapt your ideas in your mind's eye? Do you play around with your ideas or do you know right from the start what the end results will look like?

**Ben:** Usually I get an initial concept straight out, but need to develop the idea, visually and otherwise. And I've learned that it is sometimes best not to get too married to my initial concept, but allow for some change or remoulding. Because, of course, sometimes your concept doesn't fit the director's vision, and it is not always clear why. You get used to developing a concept, but not putting all your eggs in that basket. You don't want to go all the way down the road straight away, because sometimes when you do, it is very hard to explore other roads. It can be hard on the ego, but that comes with the job.

④ **Mario:** When you're working on ideas for a visual effects project, do you think first about what is and isn't technically feasible or do you simply give your imagination free rein right from the beginning?

**Ben:** I think it is very important to free the initial conceptualization and creative process from thoughts about what is technically feasible. One of the great things about working at ILM, is that we always seem to find a way to do virtually anything a director can dream up, so I like to just go for it when thinking stuff up, and then worry about how do we do this later. Sometimes you'll have to change the idea to fit what is realistically possible (or what is possible within a budget!) but you should start with a few limitations on your imagination as possible. It's much easier to find technology to fit your ideas than ideas to fit your technology.

## 3.9  Production Illustrator

Sylvain Despretz grew up in France and has used his talent for drawing as a storyboard artist and conceptual designer in the fields of advertising, television and film. Now he is one of the most sought-after conceptual artists in Hollywood and has worked on films including Alien: Resurrection, Gladiator, Black Hawk Down, Panic Room, The Fifth Element and Planet of the Apes.

①  Mario: Are you able to consciously control, summon up and influence your inner fantasy worlds and pictures? By imagining a scene and then playing it out with different variations in your imagination, for example, in order to see which one would work best?

**Sylvain:** I am able to conjure up visual pictures and retain their shapes long enough to commit them to paper crudely, but the real essence of the drawing only begins to emerge with a pencil in hand – things work graphically off of one another... Ultimately, there is generally a big difference between the point of departure and the final piece. If you press me to be more precise on the issue of 'inner imaging', I will say that I can liken the process to dreaming. In dreams, the images we see are a bit hazy, and a bit grey, and a bit imprecise. I think that on the occasions where I try to play out a scene, as you suggest, I can conjure up the opening image, but very quickly, it takes on a sort of hazy life of its own... Shapes change a bit, like a mild hallucination, and sometimes, out of the mutating form, comes another idea. Still, the process of committing all this to paper is what incarnates the idea, because the process is not mental, ultimately, but graphic. The effect of lines working against each other on paper helps generating a harmony, very much like notes do in music. One follows another, and pretty soon, you have a melody – or not. Ridley Scott told me once that he begins to see a scene in his mind, after he has drawn the first image... Not until that point can he see the next one, and so on. I think this describes the importance of 'incarnating' a mental image into a graphic form.

②  Mario: How, in detail, would you describe the pictures produced by your imagination?

**Sylvain:** I sometimes see movement, and certainly see it if I'm trying to picture something whose design is depending on movement. I tend to 'see' inner pictures in something that approximates black and white, or at least a very sombre set of colours. That's probably why I tend to overcompensate by using very rich colours in the painting phase. Mostly, those inner pictures are a bit bare, and I need to densify them quite a bit as soon as I commit them to paper, as I just explained.

③  Mario: Today, many creatives attempt to realize their ideas on screen straight from the imagination without any sketching. Do you think this is better than setting ideas down on paper and developing them first?

**Sylvain:** I can't imagine that they really are creative. A lot of incompetence passes for creativity, you know. The most obvious reason to commit the ideas to a sketch, be it a drawing or a computer image is to communicate successfully with a crew of experts who know how to make it happen. Making things happen takes time and energy. Making things happen the way you want them to be takes even more energy. Many people are afraid of committing to a sketch because they fear that in the end, this commitment will reveal how little they controlled the final result.

## 3.10  Director of Visual Effects

Volker Engel won an Oscar for his work on Roland Emmerich's action movie Independence Day. Along his work on films such as Godzilla, Moon 44 and Universal Soldier, this built his reputation as a top visual effects supervisor. Together with his longtime friend and visual effects producer Marc Weigert, he founded the production company Uncharted Territory in Los Angeles in 1999.

① **Mario:** When you're working on an idea for a film, how do you use visual thinking to develop scenes and visual effects?

**Volker:** When we were working on our film project *Coronado*, we had a lot of creative meetings with the director Claudio Faeh. We shut ourselves in a conference room for up to eight hours a day in order to develop our ideas intensively. It was in this working environment that the ideas and images for individual scenes started to come into our heads. I would describe my own mental images as very lively, three-dimensional pictures. They are usually colourful, although not always. An idea often starts with a still image, which I then build upon gradually. It's rather like a photograph in my head, and the more I develop it and tinker with it, the more it comes to life. It's interesting that the scenes I imagine often contain sound and dialogue already.

② **Mario:** Are you able to consciously control the images in your mind, in order to try out certain scenes in your imagination?

**Volker:** Yes, of course I can also consciously control my imaginings. That's really what makes it possible for me to work with artists from the animation department. When I'm sitting with an artist and we've been working on a project for hours, I can see what is there on the screen. If it isn't what I wanted, I have a clear inner picture that I can use to tell the artist how I envisage the scene progressing.

③ **Mario:** What inspires your own visual world? Where do your fantasies come from?

**Volker:** In creative meetings, I'm usually the last one to actually say anything. I usually need a little longer, just to get things sorted out in my mind. Because of this, my ideas are usually quite precise. It stimulates me in a team situation when something like a basic idea comes up. What happens next is like a relay race, with the idea being taken a little further each time. Someone grabs the idea, adds something new to it and passes it on to the next person. When we were working on the film *Coronado*, we noticed that this kind of constructive creativity helped to build up a lot of mutual trust.

④ **Mario:** Were you a daydreamer as a child, someone who would get lost in his fantasies or imagination?

**Volker:** I had vivid fantasies even when I was a boy. Perhaps that was what led me to work in film. It was a sort of outlet for me. In my first film, called *The Desert Race*, there were four cars that raced against each other in the desert. That film could be seen as a continuation of the games I played in my sandpit when I was a boy. I used to push toy cars through the sand, like other kids do. I used to think that it was a shame that you couldn't see the rest of the story being acted out the way that it was in my head. It also spoilt it for me that you could see the hand pushing the cars. Later I managed to work out how it could be done without the hand being seen, and that's how I came to work with stop-motion animation.

## 3.11 Illustrator

Paola Piglia was born in Italy and works in London and New York for international clients and magazines including Esquire, Life and the New York Times. 'No doubt Federico Fellini will be ringing the doorbell any minute,' wrote one New York journalist, astounded by Piglia's eccentric lifestyle and extraordinary illustrations.

① **Mario:** As a illustrator, you're constantly on the lookout for new visual ideas and picture worlds. How would you describe the fantasies and mental images from which this wealth of pictures is created?

**Paola:** Actively searching for ideas is an occupation that has seldom proved successful in my case. My favourite images are often created by some deeper currents outmanoeuvring my conscious efforts to conjure them up. I think of these images coming to me as visitations. They seem to materialize like visual fulgurations revealing a world itself more real than the real one.

② **Mario:** When you're looking for ideas, do you allow yourself to be inspired by the images around you? Do you flick enthusiastically through magazines or watch films or are you someone who falls back on their own inner pictures and allows themselves to be led by their own imagination?

**Paola:** Both. In the first case, not all images one uses (or in my case does not use) are inspirational ones. I often visually research a story for days or weeks compulsively, without ever using any of the material. It is almost like collecting all the images that I know are not mine to exorcize them. It is in itself an inspiring enterprise. Directors like Wong Kar-Wai or the Kubrick of *Barry Lyndon* and *The Shining*, and many others, have impressed me tremendously and certainly influenced some of my work. I also admire artists like Bill Viola or Anish Kapoor whose vision so captivates and, I hope, must rub off on my sensitivity and in my work. When ideas refuse to knock on my brain's portal as the deadline is looming, I do flick frantically through magazines as supermarkets of images, in manic search of any decent idea. It sometimes works.

③ **Mario:** This question may seem a little strange, but how, in detail, would you describe the pictures produced by your imagination?

**Paola:** A daydream is not very different from a real dream. Images appear and disappear in and out of focus. If I do not see them in my head, I see them on paper as I am drawing them. Still in the time between the brain impulse and the movement of the pencil, I think they move in slow motion to allow me to freeze on the perfect frame. Each colour invades my imagination tyrannically, No room for any images or another colour. Just monochromatic vibrancy.

④ **Mario:** At what time are you able to daydream most successfully and what particularly fires your imagination?

**Paola:** I believe any creative process needs vast expanses of time. I could not be put at a desk and work for a couple of hours at a time. I need large stretches of time, full of activities but without regulations of any type. I also find travel very conducive to imaginary thinking. Planes in particular: I love the feeling of suspension in space and time, literally and otherwise.

⑤ **Mario:** When a good idea suddenly pops up or an unusual scene or picture occurs to you, how do you then record your ideas so that you don't forget them or lose some of the detail?

**Paola:** I keep sketchbooks where I draw or write ideas. I also paste images that I find interesting. The problem is that I do not always carry one with me. In such cases I draw on whatever is available: parking tickets, napkins, etc, and then I paste it in.

## 3.12  Director

Ringan Ledwidge is one of the most talented and sought-after music video and ad directors in London.
Just a glance at his long list of awards shows why clients such as Lee, Volkswagen, Fox Sports, Adidas
and Nike are so keen to work with him. His music videos include work for bands and artists such as Travis,
Kathryn Williams, Gomez and Supersonic.

① Mario: When you're looking for new visual ideas do you turn to your imagination and inner picture worlds, or do you take your inspiration from the things around you?

Ringan: For me new visual ideas are a combination of the things around you and the way your imagination plays with them to create another reality.

② Mario: Do you believe that your imagination and inner picture worlds are important to your creativity? If the answer is yes, how important a role do they play in your work?

Ringan: Imagination is an essential part of creativity, I use it to create the world I see, one which quite often skirts the edge of reality, this could be visually, through characters, sound, music, and editing. It informs about how to look at familiar things differently.

③ Mario: How would you describe the pictures created by your imagination and your mental picture worlds?

Ringan: Ideas for me manifest themselves in many different ways. Sometimes I see something in my head as if I've already shot and edited it. Other times it can just be one image that I build on, sometimes it is just a hunch or feeling. I guess what I'm trying to say for me is that creativity has many different guises.

④ Mario: Do you think it makes sense to use one's imagination as a kind of film studio in which complete scenes can be worked out? How do you use your inner imaginative worlds to develop new ideas or play scenes through in your head?

Ringan: For every filmmaker, being able to explore ideas or scenes in your head is essential and probably varies tremendously from one individual to another. I personally use it to allow my characters to explore their world, to understand how they would react to certain situations, I guess kind of like an actors' workshop. Visually I always have strong feelings about what I want, but rather than lock them down I prefer to explore them on the day. Like a chemistry experiment, a very different reality can explode when you step onto set. That's exciting and I like to be free enough to explore it.

⑤ Mario: We are submerged by an unbelievable torrent of new and effective pictures by the media every day. Which of these pictures in your view will win the battle for the public's attention?

Ringan: Unfortunately the majority of media imagery these days is governed by research and box ticking. In my opinion the pictures that stand out are the ones in which the creator's point of view has been allowed to remain true. Unfortunately, this is becoming harder and harder to achieve.

⑥ Mario: Thanks to the computer there are no longer any limits to the imagination. Do you think creatives have already realized what unbelievable potential the computer offers or is there still something lacking in terms of fantasy and imagination?

Ringan: At the moment in filmic terms I feel that the computer still limits the imagination through a combination of filmmakers' fear of it and education. But I believe that it will eventually become a more natural part of the way we use out imagination, and create the freedom that computer games enjoy.

## 3.13  Game Developer

interview

(SHIGERU MIYAMOTO)

Shigeru Miyamoto invented video games as we know them today. He developed legendary games such as Super Mario, The Legend of Zelda and Donkey Kong and is now known as the Spielberg of the gaming world. Through countless awards and exhibitions, he remains a creative power to be reckoned with and works with Nintendo on the active development of many of their new games.

① **Mario:** You are able to look back on a unique career as games developer. Do you believe that your imagination is important to your creativity?

**Miyamoto:** The basis of my making games is constantly asking myself the question, 'How would ordinary things look if I observe them from a slightly different angle to the way we normally do?' or 'How interesting would the world be if our normal daily lives could become a bit extraordinary?' Also, I used to draw cartoons in my childhood. I had to create interesting plots and let the readers see them in the appropriate order. I believe having had such experiences in my childhood helps me create the ideas today.

② **Mario:** Many of the pictures we get to see in computer-animated films or computer games have very little to do with the real world as we know it. How do you develop pictures that no one has seen before and how do you use your imagination when searching for ideas of this kind?

**Miyamoto:** My way of making games is to start with thinking about unique ideas that cannot be realized by other forms of entertainment. In other words, aesthetic viewpoint is not the primary goal when I make game characters. They are created to carry out the ideas that I have imagined in the best way. At the same time, however, I often scribble any pictures on paper when I feel like doing so. Sometime, I gather these sketches and then think about game ideas from these pictures. For example, in the case of *Donkey Kong*, I doodled the picture of a main character dodging barrels.

③ **Mario:** Many creatives describe the process of getting ideas as a game involving inner pictures and ideas. Picture elements are often combined, scenes changed and new material added. If you were to think now about how you personally develop ideas, how would you describe the process you go through?

**Miyamoto:** Thinking about ideas in my mind is important, but even more important is for me to grab the controller and ask myself again and again if the feeling I want the players to experience is being properly reproduced there. So, emotional elements are very important for me to create new ideas, rather than making inner pictures. My way of drawing pictures is more like doodling and can even be seen as messy. My process of creating ideas sometimes follows a similar pattern.

④ **Mario:** When you are looking for ideas, do you allow yourself to be inspired by the images around you? Do you flick enthusiastically through magazines or watch films or are you someone who falls back on their own inner pictures and allows themselves to be led by their own imagination?

**Miyamoto:** I hardly ever receive inspiration from the information dispatched by others. Whenever it may be and wherever I am, I am always thinking hard about unique and interesting ideas. I discuss these new ideas with my colleagues and we actually reproduce the ideas and improve upon them. Repeating this process is the way my ideas materialize. I use big pieces of paper, on which I attach a number of different memos describing my ideas. I itemize these memos to think about the flow.

part 2

The Six Ways Of Seeing

02 part02

# The Six Ways Of Seeing

This chapter will explain the full spectrum of ways in which images can be produced by visual thinking or perceived in the real world through our senses. There are six types of seeing and almost everyone has these at their disposal in their own individual way, even if for the most part they use them intuitively and therefore with varying degrees of restriction. These six ways of seeing constitute a kind of basic kit that could be compared to an artist's studio. Everything that we need for our picture is ready and waiting, but the picture itself in all its uniqueness will depend on who is using the tools. The six ways of seeing are at the bottom of this page.

## There's no such thing as magic

The following chapter shows you how to use your eyes and your visual imagination to develop new and better creative concepts. This will enable you to take your first steps away from a purely instinctive use of images to a conscious handling of the tools of the visual trade. It may well be that the myth of creativity will lose some of its mystique in the process, but magicians do not believe in magic; they know exactly which strings to pull in order to astonish their audience. Perhaps, though, you may be asking yourself what is the point of studying something that you are going to use intuitively anyway. The object is to make you sensitive to your strengths, and to show you which areas of your imagination can be improved and expanded. This knowledge will give you the chance to develop your own gifts and to experiment with ways of increasing your creative potential. Interestingly, however, in some interviews with top creatives it transpired that they found it confusing to think about things they always do automatically and instinctively. Perhaps if you are an experienced driver, you can draw a parallel by imagining that you are driving along with a passenger, who wants to show you how to change gear in a manner that will be less wearing on the clutch. You have now been driving for so many years that you have simply never

---

**01 Looking Is Not Seeing**

How to move from mere looking to the art of seeing, so the real world becomes a source of inspiration.

**02 The World In Your Head**

How to bring the world into your visual imagination and make your images more vivid and clear.

**03 Dream With Your Eyes Open**

How to combine reality and fantasy into a creative vision and discover things that no one else can see.

the six ways of seeing

**04 Controlling Images**

Learning to control visual thinking consciously, so that you can direct the movies inside your mind.

**05 See With All Your Senses**

Learning to see with your ears and hear with your hands, using all your senses to create visual ideas.

**06 Image Streaming**

Giving more scope to your creative intuition, so that visual ideas can happen spontaneously.

bothered or needed to think about when, how or even why you need to depress the clutch. It's all done without thinking, automatically. But now the passenger explains to you that you should release the clutch earlier and quicker, particularly over the last third. On hearing this, for the first time in years you will become conscious of what you're doing, and I'll guarantee that you'll become so confused that you'll change gear as clumsily as if it were just your third driving lesson. It's completely normal to get confused when we make ourselves conscious of actions that we have always performed successfully by instinct. But if, for instance, you wanted to change from driving your family car to driving a racing car, you would have to go through precisely this phase of consciously relearning how to change gear. And so if you want to move up into a higher gear of creativity, you will need to look consciously inside yourself in order to find out how to use your potential to greater effect than before.

## Don't expect too much

Before you begin the first exercise, test your own expectations. One of the quickest routes to frustration is to have excessively high expectations both of yourself and of the results. I would therefore prefer to talk about 'ideas' rather than 'seeing'. Many people can visualize a scene in which, for instance, a man walks through a wall, but some would not regard this imagined event as 'seeing' an image, or

they would not want to use that sort of verb to describe it. You may feel that inner vision is not vivid enough, or that something isn't working properly – but it's perfectly normal for the quality to vary from person to person. For beginners especially, it's advisable to rein back your expectations and simply approach these exercises in a spirit of curiosity. Don't concentrate too hard, because pressure only creates counter-pressure, which will hinder and not help you. It's like learning to juggle. Even with three balls you have to give up trying to keep your eye on all of them, because if you do, you'll lose them all. If you want to juggle them successfully, you should not look at them. Many people, though, think that you have to watch them all closely so that you can keep them under control. This is physically impossible, because the moment you fix your eyes on one of them, the others will disappear from view. Our inner images work the same way.

If you find you're not making any progress, then start playing by the following rules: try not to see anything, but just develop some vague idea of an image. Make it part of your training not to take things too seriously. For people with high expectations this is often the most important step of all. Nobody expects you to see a particular vision, and there is nobody looking over your shoulder. For the time being at least, it doesn't matter at all how vivid these images are, and so you can even cheat a little and make up whatever bits you can't yet see. If this doesn't work, then take a break.

# 1.  Looking Is Not Seeing

When did you last look so closely at the leaves of a plant that they appeared to you in a totally new light? We often look at things without really seeing them; what we see is merely the commonplace elements, and we do not take the trouble to let our senses register all the details of what is there before us. To do that, we must make a conscious effort. Only then can we discover new things, and find inspiration by perceiving objects, organisms or situations in all the richness of their complexity. The art critic and author John Berger maintains that the way we see things is greatly influenced by what we believe and what we know. It might also be said that we only see what we know. An architect will probably wander through Vienna and see it in a completely different way from, for example, a physicist or a child. Looking is an active selection process, and we only see what we are looking at. With the following exercises, you will find out the limits of your own faculties of visual perception. You may therefore become more aware that, for instance, you can only take in a certain range of colour frequencies. This will show you where the frontiers lie, and will therefore automatically lead you into the exercises in subsequent chapters that deal with the imagination. Our eyes cannot penetrate the surface of an uneaten apple, but we can imagine what lies beneath. These exercises will help you to make a sharper distinction between exterior and interior, between the real and the imagined.

## WHAT IS THE PURPOSE OF THESE EXERCISES

›› Seeing provides the basis for all imaginary images.

›› Detailed seeing enhances drawing ability.

›› Conscious seeing opens doors into reality.

›› Seeing makes you more aware of the borders of reality and imagination.

›› Seeing can inspire you with a new vision of familiar things.

### 01  Make Your Eyes Work

Have a look at something close to you and imagine that your gaze is catching hold of it. Take it with your eyes, turn it round, play with it, feel it, and let your eyes glide over its surface. Use an active, aggressive gaze that takes what it wants; do not passively accept whatever comes. Try to bridge the gap between yourself and the object and imagine it very close to you. Discover its edges, let your gaze play over it, and look for new things, hidden details. Of course you can also do the exact opposite: look at it passively, let it work its own effects on you without imposing any desire or purpose of your own.

### 02  Focus On The Object

Look at an object and try to remodel it. Make it clearer and more defined by relegating all the things around it to the background. Turn its surroundings into a blur, so that the object itself becomes the absolute focal point of your attention. Now you will now be able to observe it in all its detail. But you should not become rigid or stare fixedly at it; instead let your eyes play over it, discovering its boundaries. If you stare at the object or fix your gaze, you will find that your attention will soon wander, and you will start wanting to look elsewhere.

Concept and Photography:
Staudinger+Franke
www.staudinger-franke.at

03 Aspects of Seeing

**Light and Shade ››**

Look at any object you like, or at the picture on the left, and ask yourself in exactly what light you are seeing it. Would its essence, its expression, its form, its colours or its meaning change if the lighting were to change? What shadows are created by the light that is falling on the object, and where exactly can you see them?

**Colours and Surface ››**

There are millions of different colours. Which of them can you distinguish at the moment when you are looking at the object? Study the surface and identify its colours and its qualities. Note their intensity, their brightness, and any other features of the colours you can see.

**Space and Perspective ››**

Whereabouts in the room is the object situated? What view do you have of it at the moment? How will its effect, its essence, its appearance be changed if you change your position or if the object is moved to another spot?

**Analysis and Synthesis ››**

Take the object apart and see how it is constructed and what it is made of. What materials have been combined into what shapes? Now try to reassemble it piece by piece.

**All in Proportion ››**

In order to perceive its proportions accurately, it can be useful to divide an object into its most important parts. What is it made of, and how is it put together? What relationship do the proportions have to one another? For instance, does the size of the wheels fit in with the overall dimensions of your car? Or is your nose proportionate to the rest of your face?

(2) The Six Ways Of Seeing    39

## 2.  The World In Your Head

How does the world get inside your head? I'd like you to answer this question for yourself, and I will show you a few exercises to help you work out the answer. You should consider them as training – a kind of introduction meant primarily for people with a limited capacity for creating inner images. But even if your ability to do this is highly developed, you can still improve it through practice, by training your mind's eye to picture the outer world with more clarity, more colour, more detail, more life.

In this respect, the exercises you have done in the first chapter link up seamlessly with those that follow, because it is only when your own vision of the world reaches its peak of richness that you will be able to reproduce images of a similar quality inside your imagination. Regard these exercises as a game, and do not treat them as a competition. In these early stages it doesn't matter how long you spend doing them – it's more important that you do them regularly and build up your skills.

### WHAT IS THE PURPOSE OF THESE EXERCISES

›› To sharpen your vision and make your images richer.
›› To make the images clearer and more lively.
›› To give your visual thinking a broader basis.
›› To improve your doodling and drawing skills.

### 01    Seeing Colours

This simple introductory exercise is meant especially for people who find it difficult to come up with imaginary images. But it will also be useful for those who can already conjure up lively scenes but can only visualize them in black and white or shades of grey. Of course this is not a problem in itself, but if you would like to bring a little more variety to your inner visions, then look for something around you that is inseparably linked to a particular colour. For example, bananas are normally yellow, and we automatically associate the leaves of most plants with the colour green. Look very closely at the object of your choice, and then try to recall it in your imagination. The object itself is not important – it is simply a means of enabling you to see its particular colour. If you can't visualize it with your eyes open, then try closing them. But you are not recommended to practise this exercise while driving your car! Try it with different colours, and apply it to different objects around you – the orange of an orange, the blue of the sky, the green of a meadow.

### 02    Seeing Afterimages

Our second exercise is just as simple and can be very rewarding even for people who have difficulty imagining pictures. Seeing afterimages is a retinal effect and not a mental one. Anyone can produce an afterimage if their eyes are in good order. All you have to do is look at an object for a certain amount of time, and then close your eyes. The impression on the retina will produce an afterimage that remains visible for a few seconds. You can then use it step by step to picture the object of your choice in your inner eye. Repeat this exercise as often as necessary to build up every detail of the object in your imagination. It's quite possible that the object will keep disappearing or changing into something else, but that's no problem – give yourself a break, and then have a go at the next exercise.

## 03 Visual Concentration

If the first two exercises have failed to produce satisfactory results, then try this one. It will bring you closer to the object and will help you to concentrate more on the image. Take your time to have a detailed look at the object that you wish to picture. Try to see it as if you had never seen it before in your life. Study it very closely, concentrating fully on the visual impressions that it makes on you. Allow your gaze to wander – as you did in the first two exercises – over its surface and all its facets. What material is it made of, how is it structured, what colours can you make

out, what is the interplay of light and shade, and where exactly are its edges?

Now close your eyes and try to reproduce the object in your mind's eye with as many details as possible. Build the image up step by step, but don't burden yourself with the expectation that you will immediately see everything as clearly as in a photograph. If that's what you want to see, then a proper photograph of the object will give you a better chance. You will, however, make far more progress if you keep focusing on the object and don't let your attention wander. This improves concentration, though it may take you quite a while. If you only achieve partial success, open your eyes and repeat the process as before.

The next step is to use your hands, if it's possible: take hold of the object and examine it using all five of your senses. The more these are brought into play,

Client: Swatch
Agency: Neogama
Creative Direction:
Alexandre Gama
Source: Lürzer's Archive 5/2002

If you don't have a suitable object near you, use the ad (right) for the exercises on this page.

Below
Client: Levi Strauss & Co
Project: TV commercial
Agency: Bartle Bogle Hegarty
Director: Jonathan Glazer
Special Effects: Framestore CFC
Creative Direction: Stephen Butler

the more your imagination will be stimulated. Then close your eyes again and see what comes up before your inner eye.

## 04 Outlines and Shapes

The next exercise is a small contribution to the overall structure of the imaginary picture. In this you will focus more on individual features and basic forms than on the picture as a whole. Look at an object and concentrate only on its outline and its general shape. Then try to imagine its outline. If you can't do so, try again with a quick glance – like the flash of a strobe light. You can even use the remote control of your TV as an aid: stay on a channel just long enough to see what the programme is, and then zap to another and try to use the afterimage to reconstruct what you saw. You don't need to add details or colours – just the outline of things.

## 05 Picture Echoes

For this exercise, it's best to use a DVD film or sequence. Watch a sequence of at most three seconds, and then try to let it pass before your mind's eye like an action replay. If you're able to visualize the scene with all its detail, then try a longer sequence. If you should find yourself watching a boring film, this is a great way to relieve the tedium. Of course you can also pass the time like this when you're waiting for something or someone, or have nothing better to do. You can simply watch short scenes or even actions that are going on around you, and then rerun them in your head.

Right
**Client:** Norwich Union
**Photography:** Ray Massey
**Agency:** The A.G.A Group
**Art Direction:** Kate Gorringe

## 06 Optical Illusions

If you think you can visualize things perfectly, here's a chance to discover your limits. The picture above was designed for an advertising campaign and uses an Escher-style optical illusion. Try to picture it in your imagination, and pay particular attention to the details around the three columns of the portico. Work out which features produce the illusion and see if you can visualize them. Incidentally, this has no relevance to your creativity – it's simply a little experiment to help you find out the limits of your imaginative capacity.

## 07 Drawing Exercises

Perhaps one of the best ways of training your visual imagination is drawing. There are two variations on this theme: either you can draw the object completely from memory, or you can analyse it in the way I've already described and then commit it to paper piece by piece. You don't need to be a Da Vinci to do this, and it's enough to begin with very simple objects.

# 3.   Dream With Your Eyes Open

You don't necessarily have to close your eyes in order to dream. On the contrary, it's often essential to go through the world with your eyes open to provide your imagination with the right surface onto which to project its imagery. In this chapter I want to give you a few interesting exercises that will show you how to project your images onto the world around you, so that you can discover ideas that are hidden from other people. Additionally, though, the exercises are meant to demonstrate how the environment can be used as a trigger to set off all kinds of fascinating associations in the imagination. This is not a magic trick – just an everyday phenomenon that most of us experience regularly.

When, for instance, we are under stress and are waiting for the taxi to take us to the airport, it can happen that we hear the doorbell even though nobody has rung. The later it gets, the stronger these illusions become. When we look out of the window, every second car seems suspiciously like a taxi, even though it isn't. Our expectations make us project these images or desires onto the real world, and very often they are almost indistinguishable from real perceptions. We use the same faculty when we look up at a deserted house and glimpse the features of a face or the shape of an animal. Another example is a New Year custom that is popular in some countries, including Germany: party guests heat up some small pieces of lead over a candle and pour the molten metal into cold water. The solidified pieces are passed around and 'interpreted'. Everyone projects their own fantasies and associations onto these amorphous lumps, and in the process reveals their own wishes, or discovers symbols that are meant to bring good fortune in the New Year. Most of us have been using this imaginative skill since early childhood, seeing monsters in the clouds, or transforming a fallen branch into a sword. It's far from unusual for young children to have imaginary playmates, and some even

put out an imaginary chair, and imaginary food and drink for their imaginary friend. Research has shown (e.g. Siegel 1993) that many children not only regard these images as real, but claim actually to have seen them in the flesh. Although we grow out of these illusions, they stem from the same faculty that enables our minds to creatively fashion the world around us. Leonardo Da Vinci used this very method well into old age, and even described it in his writings on painting: 'When you look at a wall spotted with stains, or with a mixture of stones, if you have to

## WHAT IS THE PURPOSE OF THESE EXERCISES

›› To make your imaginary pictures clearer and brighter.
›› To project these pictures onto the real world with open eyes.
›› To broaden the basis of your visual thinking and give it more flexibility.
›› To make conscious use of your imagination to change what you can see.
›› To use the real world as an inspiration for new ideas.

devise some scene, you may discover a resemblance to various landscapes, beautified with mountains, rivers, rocks, trees, plains, wide valleys and hills in varied arrangement; or again you may see battles and figures in action; or strange faces and costumes, and an endless variety of objects, which you could reduce to complete and well-drawn forms. And these appear on such walls confusedly, like the sound of bells in whose jangle you may find any name or word you choose to imagine.'

If you have studied the interviews in the first section of this book, you will know that the ability to dream with your eyes open and to project your imagination onto the real world is a vital creative strategy for many practitioners.

## Associating and Projecting

You are probably already familiar with the next exercise, but your visualization skills may be a little out of practice. Use the circles on the right as a surface on which to project your images, and try to work out what this shape could represent. It could be anything – from a bottle top to a wedding ring. Look closely at it, and try to impose your inner images onto the two circles so that you can actually see the imagined object. What associations does the shape have, what living organisms or inanimate objects have a similar shape or contain circles like these as an integral part of their design? Of course you can also change the circles if you wish to, and adapt them to your own concepts. You should come up with as many ideas as possible, and don't stop even when you reach thirty. You can take the process even further and devise a whole story around the circles. You can also change the perspective by turning the book round. You can do whatever you like and whatever seems to work. The only person who can limit what you do is you.

You can increase the difficulty level of this exercise by using a light bulb to imagine creatures or objects, as the illustrator Serge Bloch has done (left).

Illustration: Serge Bloch
Agency: Marlena Agency
www.marlenaagency.com

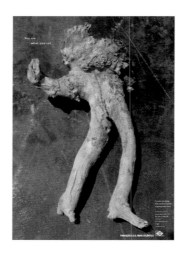

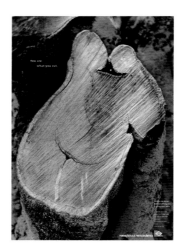

The ideas underlying the ad campaigns on these two pages have one thing in common: they all depend on our ability to see an object as something that is not actually there. You need this kind of talent for dreaming with your eyes open to be able to come up with ideas like these and to project images onto objects in a similarly creative way.

## O2    Fantastic Projections

In this exercise we shall go a step further and try to change visible things in accordance with what we can imagine. Open your eyes and look at a scene, an object or an animal, and then use your imagination to alter it. You might call this a positive hallucination. What we see is transformed by what we imagine. For instance, while you are reading this real sentence, the top left-hand corner of the page might begin to burn, or the black letters might begin to melt like wax and run down the paper. Of course you can't actually see these things, but your imagination can provide an image of what they might look like.

Children have a particular gift for this exercise, as you can often see when they're playing. With their eyes open, they can imagine scenes in which a knight, for instance, escapes from his enemies by running into the castle – which in reality is just a fenced-in vegetable patch. Try out the technique for yourself:

choose an object, and then with your eyes open manipulate it into changing its shape, falling apart, swelling, shrinking, bursting, ballooning or merging with something else. You can, of course, use the pictures on this page for practice.

## O3    Fantasy Film Projector

An interesting variation of the previous exercise is to try and imagine a short film sequence or to recall a scene that you have just been watching. Can you replay the scene in your mind's eye? If you can, find a white wall and try to project the scene onto it with your eyes open, as if you were seeing the film on the screen. This exercise is an ideal way of improving your visual capabilities and strengthening the muscles of your imagination.

Above
Campaign to save the Brazilian rainforests.
Client: Fundação SOS Mata Atlântica
Agency:
F/Nazca Saatchi & Saatchi
Art Direction: Luciano Lincoln
Photography: João Caetano

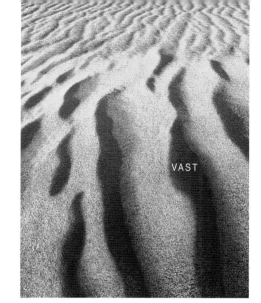

Client: Royal Velvet
Agency: McKinney & Silver
Art Direction:
Gerardo Blumenkrantz
Photography: Alexis Logothetis
Source:
Lürzer's Archive 5/2002

## O4    Automatic Drawing

It is said that for inspiration Leonardo Da Vinci used to close his eyes and let his chalk glide at random over the paper. Then he would open his eyes to see what he had drawn, and he would later use these spontaneous, chance pictures, patterns and doodles to provide him with ideas for his paintings and inventions. Nowadays, many creatives use the same improvisational technique to come up with basic ideas. They switch off their conscious control and give free rein to their pencil, in just the same way as many of us like to doodle while we're on the phone or attending a dull meeting. Try it when you're working on a new project. The results may not always be immediately evident, and they may not conform to your usual aesthetic standards, but they can still be a rich source of new ideas. Just look at the doodle, allow associations to come freely into your mind, and project your imagination into it. In this way, your subconscious mind will create raw material for your conscious mind to work with – this can be a rich source of ideas and an excellent way of training your visual imagination.

'Over 100 million children live
on the street. And eat from it.'
Client: Unicef
Agency: Springer & Jacoby
Art Direction: Bettina Olf
Photography: Jan Burwick

# 4.   Controlling Images

For creatives, what is more important than the clarity or realism of imaginary images is the ability to control them. This ability has several important functions. It enables us to reconstruct ideas in our head, and to improve, supplement or extend them by experimenting with typography, figures and many other devices. It gives us the chance to do a test run with our images, which not only can save time but can also prevent us from making expensive mistakes. Together with doodling, it is an indispensable tool. Even before you sit down at the computer, you will have a very definite vision of what the end product should look like.

Alfred Hitchcock already knew in advance most details of his films, including the lighting, the camera angles and the editing. Once the film had been edited, there were very few metres of unused material. We too can visualize whole scenes in our mind's eye, like Spider-Man swinging between skyscrapers, and we can also change them. In this sense, your imagination can supply you with a complete film and post-production studio, and in turn you can stage the most spectacular and outrageous special effects that have ever been seen. The same, of course, applies to the fields of graphic design, photography, illustration, architecture and animation. It is strange that many creatives still haven't quite cottoned on to the vast new range of possibilities. The following exercises are therefore designed to help you discover how well you can consciously guide your images, and how freely you can allow your own inner stream of ideas to flow. For on the one hand, we need control so that we can deliberately tailor our stories and scenes to our requirements, but on the other hand, the free and spontaneous flow of ideas is essential if our intuition is to provide us with the amount of imaginary raw material that we need.

## What has concentration got to do with imagination?

The ability to concentrate is probably the most important talent you'll need if you are to make full use of the exercises contained in this chapter. Creatives have often described the strain of maintaining their mental images. If you just picture the dashboard of your car, you might be able to

### WHAT IS THE PURPOSE OF THIS EXERCISE

›› To mould daydreams and fantasies into new ideas.
›› To create more detailed images and to guide them consciously.
›› To save time and trouble by trying out ideas in your head.
›› To train your creative skills and allow your imagination to take flight.

visualize, say, the speedometer, the clock and the petrol gauge, but very few people can picture it in its entirety. Even when we are looking at the real thing, some parts will stand out more clearly while others will sink into the background in a kind of blur.

Most of these exercises require concentration, but you may notice that after a few minutes your attention will begin to wander, and you'll want to start thinking of other things. You may find yourself confronted by an inner flow of images or dialogues that try to distract you from the exercise. Just let them go. Try not to hold onto them, and stop them from taking over.

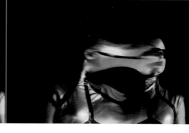

OI    **Movies In Your Mind**

The following exercise gives you instructions on how to consciously manipulate a short film sequence that you are projecting onto the imaginary screen of your mind's eye. The challenge lies in repeating and deliberately guiding the scene you have selected. It might, for example, be a personal experience from the past, an idea for a TV ad, a comic scene from a film you've seen recently, or you can simply use the illustration on this page. Try to picture a clear sequence, and pretend that you can alter this imagined scene in the same way that you would edit it on the computer or in the cutting room.

- Colour the scene or make it black and white.
- Try to fast-forward it.
- What sort of soundtrack is there?
  Can you make it louder, or change the pitch?
- Make the picture sharp. Now turn the controls in the other direction and make it blurred.
- Change the size of the picture, or the content.
- Stop the film and freeze the image.
- Let the film run backwards.
- Can you see yourself in this scene?
  What role are you playing?
- Can you enlarge one section of the picture, or make it smaller?
- Change the perspective. Change the order of events.
- What else can you experiment with?
  What else can you change?

Artist: Louise
Song: Beautiful Inside
Project: Music video
Special Effects: Glassworks Ltd
Creative Direction: Stephen Butler

 **From Stills Into Movies**

There are some people who can develop very clear mental images, but only as stills. What are your own visual worlds like? Do they usually consist of moving pictures, scenes, whole stories? For this exercise you should try to transform the picture above back into the music video from which it is taken. Breathe life into it and visualize how the scene might continue. This will stimulate your imagination and strengthen your inner eye.

feel was missing? Would there be a lot of people in it, or would there be more scenes and landscapes mixed with objects that you are always looking at? Would your audience be confronted with strong emotions or with something wishy-washy and dull? What might others see in your film that they normally don't see themselves? Let an imaginary video of today run before your inner eye, and enjoy yourself!

**03  Video Surveillance**

The idea for this exercise comes from the creativity trainer Tom Wujec. If you want to become more aware of the things you focus on in everyday life, you should stop and ask yourself precisely what it is that you *do* focus on. If you were to capture all these everyday scenes, objects and people on film or video, what would an audience make of them? What would they regard as excessive in your film, and what would they

**04  Panoramic Views**

For the following exercise it might be useful to close your eyes in order to shut out the distractions of the outside world. Choose a short scene from one of your favourite films and imagine yourself caught up in it. When you can see the picture clearly, pan slowly left, as if your head were a camera. What can you see that is not visible in the film? Do you know what is behind you on the right? If you don't, turn your head and have a good look at the scene that meets your eyes.

Above
Artist: TIGA
Song: Hot in Herre
Project: Music video
Label: !K7 Records
Production: Eyeball NYC
Creative Direction: Limore Shur

Above right
The look of an illustration was
created by superimposing a real
car on a painted studio set.
Photography: Dietmar Henneka
Client: DaimlerChrysler AG
Set Construction:
Peter Boeck & Team
www.henneka.com

## 05 Sensing What You Can't See

Use your imagination to transform intuitive or instinctive perceptions into imaginary pictures. For example, what do you think is happening fifty metres behind you? Do you have a feeling about it, and can you visualize it without turning around? Play about with these instincts. Try to picture what might lie two metres below your feet. What might be going on down there right now? Make a mental picture of it, or conjure up a whole scene. Go down into the earth, walk through walls, dive into the water, pass through people, build up a scene involving everything within a certain radius of yourself.

## 06 Playing Around With Styles

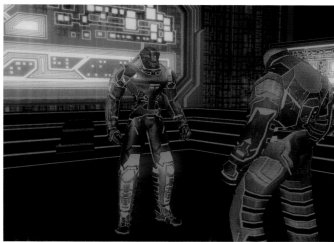

TRON® Owned by Cooper Industries, Inc. and used by permission. ©Disney

Look at the three pictures on the right, and try to distinguish the salient features of their style: collage, animation and illustration. Now look around you and choose a scene that you find interesting. Try to imagine this scene captured in one of those three styles. What would be the effect on the objects, people and setting if the whole scene were transformed in this manner?

You can try this out with your eyes open simply by looking at your chosen scene and imagining it in your chosen style. But if you find it easier, close your eyes and do the same thing with the scene as you remember it. There are no limits to what your imagination can visualize. Picture the scene as part of a silent movie of the 1920s, or as a Van Gogh painting, or turn it into a collage of old newspapers.

You don't necessarily have to see the whole picture transformed – it's enough just to have an idea of how a change of style can change both an image's appearance and its effect.

Centre right
Computer Game: Tron 2.0
Publisher: Buena Vista Games
Developer: Monolith

Below right
Client: Comedy Central
Production: Eyeball NYC
Creative Direction: Limore Shur

## 07 Mindgate

Conjure up a picture before your mind's eye – maybe a landscape from *Lord of the Rings*, or a place you haven't been to for a long time. When the picture is clear in your mind, look at it with some detachment, as if it were a painting hanging on a wall. Try to ensure that any distracting elements close to you are relegated to the background. Now zoom in on the picture so that you can make out every detail. Next, try to cross the threshold and go into the picture yourself. Does it take on breadth and depth? When you can move around freely inside it, look at the landscape. You may soon discover that the picture is larger than you had thought when you first observed the scene. Now turn round and look back into the room from which you first entered the picture. Can you see only the room, or can you see yourself too?

## 08 Rehearsal Studio

Try to imagine as vividly as possible the scene shown in the images below as a film sequence. If it doesn't work with that scene, then choose a different scene from memory or from a DVD.

Now, in your imagination, change one small detail from the sequence. Don't make any radical changes, but simply alter one feature – either by leaving it out, adding something to it, or combining it with a new feature. Take your time, and proceed in stages if you like. Next you will be able to imagine how the scene might be improved. What is missing, what shouldn't be there, what is original about it, what would surprise, shock or amuse an audience? Play around with this scene in your imagination until you have transformed it to your own liking and feel that you now know every aspect of it.

## 5.   Seeing With All Your Senses

In the preceding sections, we have dealt with four ways of seeing, all of which involved only the visual side of our imaginations. I expect some readers will have found this irritating, because visual images are normally accompanied by four other senses: hearing, touch, smell and taste. Hearing plays a particularly important part, as many fantasies and daydreams are almost inconceivable without an inner dialogue or, at least, monologue. Some creatives have developed their own individual methods of producing visual ideas using texts they read or write down. In this process too, what happens is that texts are heard inwardly and then, as with reading a novel, are refashioned into a visual form.

Hearing can also play an important part as an outer or inner stimulus for new ideas. Walt Disney, after making his animated film *Fantasia*, described his inspiration by saying 'When I heard the music it made pictures in my head.' We take music and visualize the stories that it seems to awaken in our imagination. It's like watching a concert. At some time or another, almost everyone has experienced the power of music to stimulate the imagination and to release a flood of images. Many people use music in the same way that they might use books, to stir up their imaginations and to transport themselves to another world.

But for visual thinking, our emotions are just as important as our hearing. You can be quite certain that your fantasies and daydreams will almost always be accompanied by emotions, even if you are not necessarily aware of them. For some people, they are so vital that they are a prerequisite for the production of any imagined reality. Others consider that images unaccompanied by emotion are valueless. Their feelings tell them exactly whether their ideas are 'right' or not. A good feeling will tell you whether an image conveys the atmosphere you need and whether it will lead to the result you want. And just like music and inner dialogues, emotions can also produce ideas. Personally, I always need to move around and establish a certain physical feeling before I can start working mentally. Others say that the best ideas come to them when they're playing games or when they're

### WHAT IS THE PURPOSE OF THESE EXERCISES

›› To extend visual thinking to all your senses.
›› To discover new sources of inspiration.
›› To get to know and develop your own creative strategies.
›› To expand your creative abilities as broadly as possible.

out in the countryside. All these examples show that stimuli for our imagination can come both from within ourselves and from outside, through our senses. The fact that the sense of sight is not the only stimulus is obvious to anyone who really understands the way that the human mind and imagination work. Take a moment to think about the role that hearing, touch, smell and taste play in your own creative work. By doing so, you will have learned something new about your own way of creating new ideas.

Title: Dreamscenes
Client: Showtime Network Inc.
Art Direction: Maud Gravereaux,
Christina Black
Post-Production and Production:
velvet mediendesign
Director and Designer:
Matthias Zentner
www.velvet.de

## OI    Playing With Sensory Filters

The purpose of this exercise is to make you more aware of which of the senses you already make good use of in your inner world, and which of them you tend to neglect. You can visualize a still scene, or run a sequence or an entire film before your mind's eye. While you do this, gradually try to establish which of your senses, apart from sight, you are using in your imaginary world. What, for instance, can you hear when the film is running? Are the imaginary pictures accompanied by imaginary dialogue? What can you feel, smell or taste? What colours can you see, and what happens when you play with them? Experiment with these different parameters, and see what it is that you change. You will observe that the more senses you integrate into your imagined scenes, the more lively and the more complete these scenes will become. You should treat the exercise as a game, but you should also pay attention to what you have to do in order to ensure that the flow of images maintains its impetus and its source of inspiration. The chart below shows the sensory parameters that you can shift to stimulate your inner visual world. You should do this exercise in a quiet and relaxed environment, somewhere where you will not be disturbed.

## O2    Feeling Images

Imagined pictures often seem incomplete and lifeless, because they lack vital elements such as sound, smell or tangibility. It follows that the more sensory your images are, the more complete and lively they will seem. For this exercise, take an object in your hand – perhaps one that you see every day but have never looked at very closely. Don't focus directly on it, but look straight ahead and examine it with your hands. If you find it easier, close your eyes. Try to imagine what the object looks like. Then integrate one sense after another into the mental image. What does the object feel like? What is its surface texture, and its temperature? What noise does it make if you drop it on the table? Notice how the image changes

| SIGHT | SOUND | TOUCH, FEEL | SMELL, TASTE |
|---|---|---|---|
| Brightness<br>dark – light | Volume<br>loud – soft | Intensity<br>hard – soft | Strength<br>strong – weak |
| Size<br>large – small | Pitch<br>high – low | Area, Extent<br>large – small | Strength<br>sweet – sour |
| Colour<br>black & white – coloured | Tone<br>clear – unclear | Texture<br>rough – smooth | Strength<br>mild – spicy |
| Picture Quality<br>contrast – saturation | Tempo<br>slow – fast | Characteristics<br>prickly – tickly – soft | |
| Focus<br>sharp – blurry | Distance<br>near – far | Temperature<br>hot – cold | |
| Movement<br>distance – direction | Rhythm<br>fast – slow | Weight<br>heavy – light | |
| Perspective<br>angle – steepness | Dimension<br>stereo – mono | Duration<br>constant – intermittent | |

each time you add another sensory impression. Does the image become clearer, are you suddenly aware of more details, and does the picture now seem fuller and more lively?

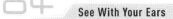

## Imagining Sense Impressions

This is an interesting variation on the previous exercise. Look at an object from a distance and concentrate on those aspects of it that you cannot perceive with your eyes. As you look at it, try for instance to form an impression of how heavy it is. Try to sense how its surface would feel – rough or smooth - and how hot or cold it might be if you were to take it in your hands. What might it sound like if you were to hit it with a piece of metal or wood? What sort of mess would the material make if you broke it? Have you any idea how it might smell? Step by step you can integrate your imaginary perceptions into your overall image of the object. You can do this exercise with your eyes open or closed. By repeating it several times, you will find out whether these images do or don't become richer and livelier.

## See With Your Ears

Listen for a moment to all the sounds around you. What can you hear? Pick out one noise after another, and let them trigger off spontaneous images in your mind's eye. Don't try to construct pictures or force them into your mind, but just relax, stay passive, and let them surprise you. It might be helpful to keep your eyes closed.

If you generally have problems with sounds, find a suitable environment and try the same exercise with music. It can be particularly stimulating to listen to beautiful multilayered compositions – the classics, for instance, or the soundtrack of a film. What comes into your mind? Is it single images, scenes, an entire film? Is it memories, or do you conjure up some vision that doesn't exist in reality? Some people see abstract coloured patterns and others slip into a stream of images that move freely and often seem unconnected to each other. Don't try to interpret your images, don't try to evaluate them, and if there are other people with you, don't make qualitative comparisons. The point of this exercise is to use acoustic stimuli in order to produce your own mental images, and to find out what it is that will trigger the flow of these images and keep it going.

## 05     Synaesthetic Visualization

The ability of the senses to overlap – known as synaesthesia – can inspire the imagination. The following exercises will show you ways of using this sensory overlap to find new visual ideas. See what happens if you try to visualize feelings, atmospheres, sounds, smells or tastes. Fewer than one per cent of people are able from birth to make this transition from one sense to another. Synaesthesia involves things like seeing a square when you hear an opera singer, or having a bitter taste when you look at certain numbers.

All of us, however, do possess this ability to a small degree, as is evident from some common turns of phrase: a piercing scream, biting cold, a sweet voice, a sour face. We can follow these concepts intuitively, although strictly speaking they make no sense. Try it for yourself by answering the following questions, not by trying to use logic but by going with your instincts:

- Which is louder: 6 or 3?
- Which is colder: pleasure or fear?
- Which tastes sweeter: red or blue?

If you have managed to prevent yourself from rationalizing, you will probably have found convincing answers. You will have switched from one sense to another and thus produced a kind of synaesthesia. Now try the following exercises to develop your ability to produce images on this particular level.

**01**   Visualize a positive feeling. For instance, try to see an image of astonishment or love. But put aside images that conjure up a particular face or a pair of lovers. You should instead concentrate on imagining an abstract picture of these emotions, and see what shapes and colours are conjured up.

**02**   Try to create a mental picture of how the following sounds might look – but you can visualize a whole scene if you wish:
- a cold noise
- a sweet-and-sour rustling

**03**   Apply the following objects as instructed, and turn your sensations into visual compositions without looking at the objects themselves:
- a wire brush on the skin
- an ice cube in the mouth

**04**   Try to visualize a clear picture of the smell or taste of the following without seeing them:
- cigarette smoke
- the taste of cheese

# 6.   Image Streaming

When you want to develop your ideas or give free rein to your fantasies, your surroundings are very important. As you may know from experience, most people are more open to inspiration when they are relaxed and have nothing in particular on their minds. During conversations with participants in my training courses, I've learned about the astonishing range of places where the best ideas spring into being. They all had one thing in common: they were conducive to relaxation. Long car journeys, the bathroom, the beach, playing games, sitting alone in a pub, just before going to sleep, daydreaming, sitting on the toilet. There are countless examples of people who find their inspiration from wonderfully creative acts as the morning shave, the jog in the park, the journey to work – all of them providing just the right amount of mind-numbing to pave the way for the sudden Big Idea.

Nolan Bushnell, who founded Atari in 1971, began the first video game revolution by developing the game *Pong*. The idea came to him when he was lying on a beach. You could draw up an endless list of examples like this, and the quintessential common denominator that links all these success stories is quite simply this: an uncompromising insistence on taking it easy, so that you can give yourself the time and the space to daydream! It may well be that you have shown yourself capable of coming up with the goods even under stress, but if you want to expand the range of your creativity, and get to know new sides of your talent, then you will find it well worth your while to approach things from a different angle. Relax.

Try to organize your work environment in such a way that you won't be disturbed by idle chatter, and you can occasionally get away from the blessings of modern telecommunications. Reduce the level of outside interference so that the inner flow of images will have a better chance of becoming vividly present in your mind. The fact that this idea works is confirmed by the so-called 'Ganzfeld phenomenon'. In this experiment, human guinea pigs were shut off from the outside world by having their eyes and ears blocked with special gadgets. The longer they remained isolated from external stimuli, the more active their inner perceptions and images became,

## WHAT IS THE PURPOSE OF THESE EXERCISES

›› To show how relaxation can be a creative resource.

›› To show how your environment can influence your creativity.

›› To show how you can spur your imagination to come up with new ideas.

›› To show how you can give your intuition greater freedom.

and many of these had all the intensity of the real thing. The simplest way to achieve a similar effect is to learn methods of relaxation. These will help you to shut out the pressures of the outside world and to focus on the inner, mental processes. The exercises in this chapter have two aims: firstly, to enable you to find out what sort of framework you need in order to develop your creativity to maximum effect, and secondly to show you some ways of relaxing, so that creative ideas and images can flow spontaneously into your mind.

## 01     The Best Place To Be

Do you know when, where and with whom you can best nurture your creativity? Have you actually sat down to work out which is the right environment for your own particular imagination? Use the following exercise to find out exactly what factors are most inspirational for you. Think back to a concrete situation in which you had a great idea and where you felt at your most creative. Your answers to the following questions will help you to build up a kind of map charting the terrain that is best for you. It will only take you ten minutes, but it could save you years.

### Environment and people

Where and when are you at your creative best, and most able to work on your mental images? What are your surroundings like? Are you alone then, or with other people? Who is near you at these moments? Are you in or away from your workplace? What time of day is it? Is there any special place that particularly inspires you?

### Behaviour and actions

What are you doing when inspiration strikes? How would a colleague know that you are working creatively at any particular moment? What actions and reactions are necessary in your moments of creativity? What is your body doing at those times? What are your hands doing? What is the main difference between your hands working creatively and your hands working non-creatively?

### Knowledge and skills

What specialist information do you have at your disposal at these times? What kind of knowledge inspires your creativity? Are there any particular skills that help you reach a creative peak?

### Assumptions and beliefs

During especially creative periods, what are you certain of? What do you think of the brief you have been given? What do you think of your solutions to any problems? What do you think of your own creative abilities at these times?

## 02     Relax and Pay Attention

Relaxation is a wonderful means of giving space to your fantasies and daydreams; it enables you to concentrate more on the inner world of ideas. As we have already seen, many of us automatically enter this inner world when we're performing monotonous activities like bathing or driving. They lull us into daydreaming, planning for the future, playing around with unusual ideas. Relaxation does not mean losing control, so much as consciously – but spontaneously – shifting our focus from outside events to inner contemplation. Although of course you are the world's leading expert on what makes you feel relaxed, I would nevertheless like to give you a few tips that might make it a little easier for you to achieve this desirable state. For example, it is obviously helpful if you can start off in quiet and private surroundings. Initially it can be quite hard to relax because the very fact that you are concentrating on doing so can actually block the whole process. If you have difficulty letting go, it might help you to close your eyes so that your attention can focus inwardly instead of outwardly. Here are three methods you can use.

○ The simplest way to reduce stress levels and to get yourself to relax is deep breathing. We breathe between 20,000 and 25,000 times a day to provide our bodies with oxygen and energy. The problem, however, is that we often breathe too shallowly, and this in itself can cause tension. If you spend just one or two minutes quietly and evenly taking deep breaths of air into your lungs, so that your stomach moves regularly in and out, this will help you to counter the effects of stress both physically and psychologically.

Breathe through your nose right down into your stomach, filling your lungs from top to bottom, and then breathe slowly out through your mouth. This will make you concentrate on the flow of air. But try to become a detached observer rather than consciously forcing yourself to breathe. You can help yourself by imagining that you are inhaling peace and quiet, and exhaling stress and tension. Once you have attained a degree of relaxation, you can gradually turn your attention to your inner imaginative world, and see what new ideas present themselves to your mind's eye. In this situation you can begin to play around with the tasks you have in hand, and experiment with different solutions.

○ Another way of relaxing is through music. Here too it's advisable to find a quiet spot and to get your body into a comfortable position. Choose a piece of music that will in itself radiate a certain calmness but will also stimulate the imagination. While you are enjoying it, you may also find it useful to spend a little time doing the breathing exercise. Take note of any thoughts or images that pass through your mind, but don't try to force them or develop them. Only when you feel you have achieved a certain degree of relaxation should you start thinking about particular tasks and playing around with concrete images.

○ A third means of driving away the tension is by way of everyday activities that make no special demands on our mental faculties. Many people can achieve this state through physical movement – swimming, jogging, cycling. Others may get there by washing the car, doing the ironing, attending to odd jobs round the house. Find out which activities help you most to get into the right state of mind for entering the inner world of ideas. To reinforce the effectiveness of this type of activity, you can combine it with the methods already described: when you're jogging or doing your odd jobs, take your music with you, and do your deep breathing. When you have eventually managed to switch your mind off, you will then be fresh enough to turn your attention back to specific tasks, and you will be able to tune into the stream of ideas that flows from your unconscious mind.

part 03

The Visual Lab

part03

# The Eight Departments In The Visual Lab

**TEN-SECOND SUMMARY**    These eight sections will act as a creative partner that will help you to train your visual thinking and to nurture your creative talents, and they will also serve as a visual laboratory in which you can experiment with and develop exciting new ideas.

### Creative meetings that won't kill off your ideas

Normally you set about finding new ideas on your own or as a member of a team, but maybe you'd like to try something different. How would it be if I were to become your creative partner? My task will be to ask you a number of unusual questions, which you can then use as a starting point for new journeys into previously unexplored territories of visual thinking.

Questions provoke, and if you make a serious attempt to answer them, you will automatically begin a process of searching. What does the petrol cap of your car look like? In order to answer, you will have to conjure up a mental image of the object. How would you take it off if it got stuck? To answer this one, you'll have to act out different solutions in your head. In the same way, you'll be able to use the many questions I ask you as a spur to send you off on a creative quest. Take a question you find interesting, and spend some time on it. Try and find as many different answers as you can before you move onto the next question. The longer you stay with one subject, the more deeply you will immerse yourself in the creative process.

As we are now in a laboratory situation, we shall be experimenting with images, thoughts, ideas and fantasies. It will be like doing a jigsaw puzzle. In your imagination, you will be combining the individual pieces, with each one fitting into a suitable position to bring you closer to the picture you are trying to complete. This way of proceeding has many positive advantages. My questions will probably stimulate you, but I will never prematurely criticize or shoot down your ideas. On the contrary, I intend to stay in the background, and no matter how unrealistic your ideas may seem, you will have my full support. This is important, because people with a genuinely new idea, people willing to cross boundaries, will often find themselves in a minority of one. But in this lab you can test everything that might, at a normal departmental meeting, seem too daring, too crazy, or too much of a challenge. Nobody will be looking over your shoulder here, and nobody will be censoring your ideas.

Incidentally, you may find it worth your while to use the six ways of seeing that we covered in Part 1.

### What is your goal, and what are you looking for?

Before you start, it might be useful to consider exactly what direction you want to take. In concrete terms, what are you after, what solutions are you hoping to find to which problems, and what is this all about? Are you seeking ideas for an ad campaign, a way of creating a special effect, a way to develop a character? Can you formulate your goal in one short sentence? Your goal might, for instance, be something like this: How can I make my audience aware that a blind man can see telepathically? Or maybe this: How can I show in an ad that, with this new washing powder, the colours will not fade but will retain their brightness? If you are dealing with computer games, the question might be: What would be the outer appearance of a character who goes against all the laws of nature but for this very reason is helpful to us human beings?

As you can see, we are looking for a precise, clearly defined goal. Don't try to pack everything you know about the project into this one sentence. The ideal formula is like a good title for a book – a snappy indication of what it's all about. The task is to reduce all the complex information that you have about the project into one simple sentence. This is not so much a restriction as a filter through which your attention must pass on its way to the required end. You will need to blinker your mind's eye in order to head in the right direction, because otherwise you will probably lose your way.

### Trust your images

The point of this exercise is not to reproduce, copy or plagiarize the old familiar ideas and styles, but to create new ones of your own. Don't be timid. You can attack the problem as radically as you like, step across known frontiers, and come up with things that have never been seen before. Trust implicitly and exclusively in your own fantasies and ideas, for in this book you will find not only possibilities that have already been used elsewhere, but also an awareness that there is an infinite number of ideas still waiting to be discovered.

**Make your thoughts visible**

Ideas are transient – they come, and within seconds they vanish in the stream of our thoughts. If you are a professional, you will know how vital it is to have drawing materials at hand while you are thinking, so that you can give tangible form to whatever may surface. Some people prefer to draw quick doodles, while others like to write things down in words. For years I have used a Dictaphone to record my ideas. Whatever your choice may be, always make sure that you have some means of grasping the vision. Now you have everything you need to make maximum use of our lab, so step inside. Here is a quick plan of the eight departments.

**01  A New View of Reality**

How to use unusual and original views of reality to open up new visual realms.

**02  What Are Pictures Made Of?**

How to experiment with pixels, dots and picture elements to create new images.

**03  Playing With Layers**

How to play with spatial and pictorial layers to create surprising new meanings.

the eight departments

**04  When Graphics Meet Images**

How to link text and graphic elements with images in exciting and innovative ways.

**05  Expanding Reality**

How to combine the artificial and the real to create fantastic new worlds and ideas.

**06  Morphing and Shape-Shifting**

How shifts and changes can lead to new meanings and surprising visual impressions.

in the visual lab

**07  Worlds Without Frontiers**

How fantasies can transcend the rules of reality and create worlds that have never been seen before.

**08  Styles, Trends and Genres**

How combining, connecting and mixing different styles and genres can produce something original.

# 1.   A New View Of Reality

If you want to get a new perspective on familiar objects, people or situations, you must be prepared to experiment and follow new directions. You need to be ready to play around a little more!

How can you extract new meanings from old objects? How can you depict them in a way that will suddenly make them seem unfamiliar? This chapter will place enormous emphasis on getting away from the norm and creating a new focus. 'You have to know the rules in order to break them' is a line often quoted in this context. But if you simply break the rules, you are still trapped in their regulatory framework. Truly original ideas often come from people who simply don't realize that what they are doing has been deemed impossible. So just occasionally you can allow yourself the luxury of pretending you know nothing – liberate yourself for a moment from all your specialist knowledge and experience.

The examples on the following pages will show you a few directions in which you can steer your visual thinking in order to see the world through new eyes. The main purpose here is not to manipulate reality or images with the computer, but to change the viewing perspective so that your eyes can seize on a new interpretation of reality. Take a good look and you'll be amazed by the extraordinary variety of visual ideas that can be developed simply by showing things in a new perspective.

Left and opposite, above
Client: Marithé François Girbaud
Agency: Air
Art Direction: David Loretti
Creative Direction: Tho Van Thran
Source:
Lürzer's Archive 6/2001

## SPACE AND MOVEMENT

Is there an angle from which the object has never been seen before? Could this be put to some specific, practical use? Can the situation or the object be shown from different angles at the same time? How can the object be placed so that it will be seen in a totally new light? Where could you stand to see the object in a different way? How could you adjust the space or perspective to create a new view?

Right
**Photography:** Tim Flach
www.timflach.com
**Client:** the Pavement
**Agency:** Roundel Design

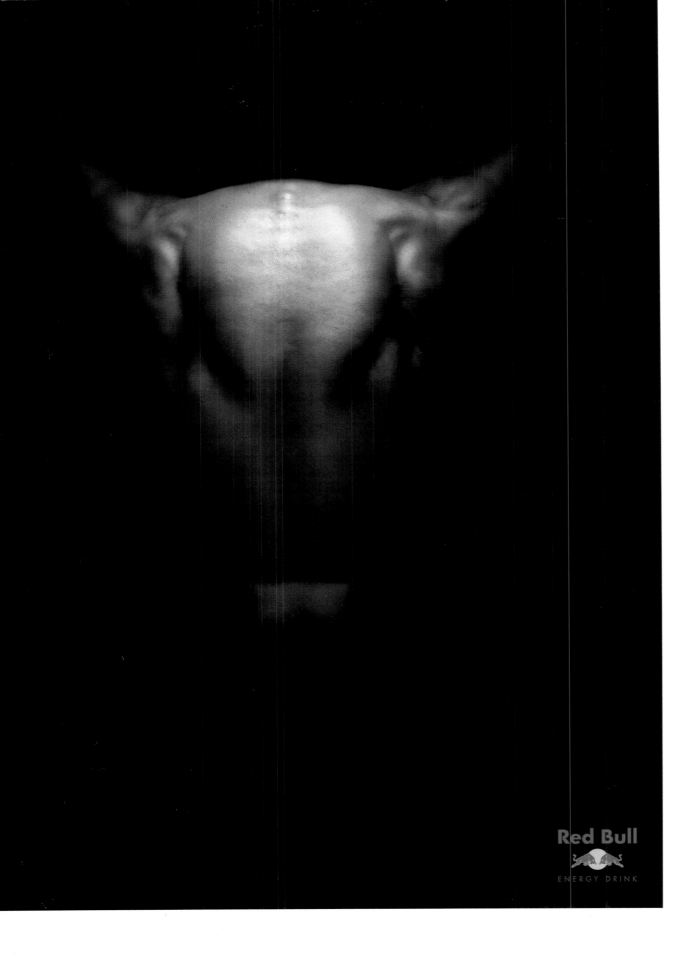

**Red Bull**
ENERGY DRINK

Client: Allexcel Trading
Product: Red Bull
Agency: Leo Burnett
Creative Direction: Tay Guan Hin
Art Direction: Sachin Ambekar
Photography: Sachin Ambekar

Above right
Photography: Paul O'Connor
www.thewalcotstudio.co.uk


Below right
Photography: Tim Flach/
Getty Images
www.timflach.com
www.gettyimages.com

## PLAYING WITH ANGLES

Does the importance of the object
change when the angle is changed?
Does its importance change when
you move or it moves? What extreme
perspectives could you adopt?
You could show just a part of the
object, or the most important aspect.
How far can it be reduced before
it becomes unrecognizable?

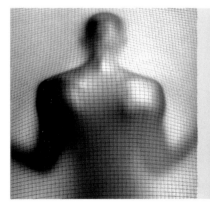

Using your eyes alone, lift something
out into the foreground. How could
you make one detail especially
prominent? How could you make
someone's view of an object
alienating, disturbing or misleading?
What can you look through in order
to make the object seem strange:
a microscope, a kaleidoscope,
sunglasses, the bottom of a glass?

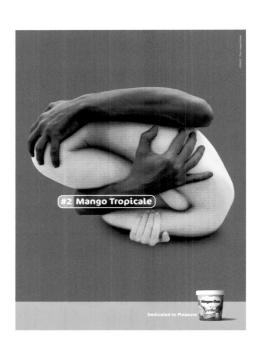

Above left
Client: Pillsbury/Haagen Dazs
Agency: Leo Burnett
Creative Direction:
Shapoor Batliwalla
Art Direction: Tone Walde
Photography: Howard Schatz

Below left
Photography: Carli Hermès
www.carlihermes.com
Client: G-Star

Basic instinct

Client: Pedras Salgadas
Agency: Bassat Ogilvy
Creative Direction: Jaume Monés
Photography: Joan Garrigosa
Source:
Lürzer's Archive 1/2002

## PLAYING WITH OBJECTS

How can bodies and objects be moulded in order to open up new perspectives? Allow them to take on and change their own shapes. What unusual and surprising views might they produce? How can objects and bodies mould each other in order to take on new significance? In what ways might they complement each other or merge into one another?

Client: Jägermeister
Agency: Philipp und Keuntje
Creative Direction: Hans Esders
Art Direction: Raphael Milczarek
Photography: Andreas H. Bitesnich

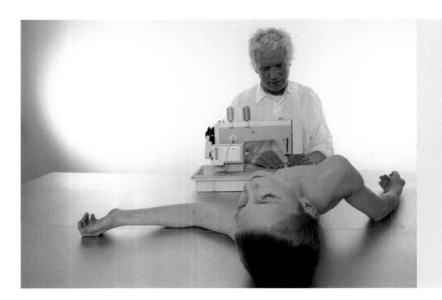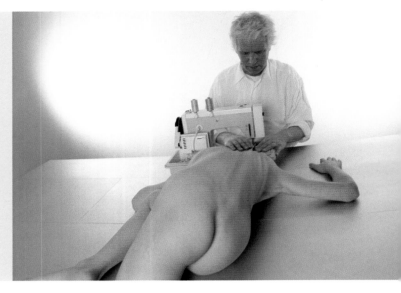

## TWISTING AND TURNING

Try rotating an object in all directions. What effect does this have? When Steven Spielberg was working on the film *Close Encounters of the Third Kind*, he called for a break and went up to the top of Hollywood Hill in order to look at the bright lights of Los Angeles. Without any particular purpose in mind, he looked at the city from a headstand position, and it was this that inspired the design of the movie's spaceship, which does indeed resemble an illuminated city upside down.

## CHANGING ROLES

Open up new perspectives by adopting the perspective of other creatures or objects. How would a bottle see the person who is drinking from it? How would a housefly see the person who is hunting it? Put yourself in the position of any object or creature in this way, and look at the world through its eyes. Use these positions to discover new angles and new images.

Left
Photography: Carli Hermès
www.carlihermes.com

Left
**Photography:** Margi Geerlinks
'Gepetto I'
www.margigeerlinks.com
www.torchgallery.com

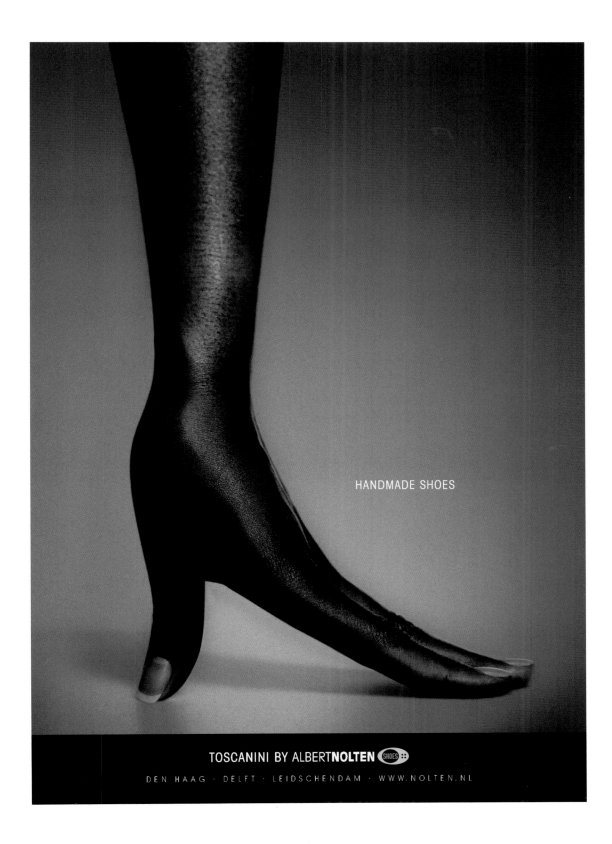

HANDMADE SHOES

TOSCANINI BY ALBERT**NOLTEN** SHOES ::

DEN HAAG · DELFT · LEIDSCHENDAM · WWW.NOLTEN.NL

Right
**Client:** Albert Nolten Shoes
**Agency:** Yokyor
**Creative Direction:** Ralph Wilmes
**Photography:** Edo Kars
**Source:** Lürzer's Archive 1/2002

Client: Spade Magazine
Agency: Ogilvy & Mather
Creative Direction: Steve Hough
Photography: Jimmy Fok
Source:
Lürzer's Archive 4/2002

Parmalat light milk. 0% fat.

✳ parmalat

Above right
Client: Parmalat
Agency: Del Campo Nazca
Saatchi & Saatchi
Creative Direction: Pablo Batlle
Photography: Maestri-Rambo
Source: Lürzer's Archive 5/2002

Below right
Client: Pino Carina
Agency: Reid Bell
Photography: Yuri Dojc
www.yuridojc.com

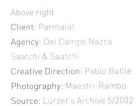

Above and left
**Photography:** Ric Frazier
www.frazierproductions.com
**Client:** Syncros Bicycles
**Agency:** Smith, Smith, Smith

For a Burberry commercial, the company's 2D logo was transformed into a 3D space through which the viewer was made to travel. In this way, a change of perspective can lead to a permanent change of meanings. At one moment the lines can be used to indicate rain, to show how the garments can withstand the weather, but then they can be transformed into a street, a building or a window.

**Above right**
Client: Burberry
Agency: Springer & Jacoby
Director: Griff
Post-Production: Studio aka

**Below right**
Client: Land Rover
Agency: Rainey Kelly Campbell
Roalfe / Y&R
Art Direction: Richard Denney
Photography: Ashton Keiditsch

Above left
Fly magnified 30 times
Below left
Velcro fastener magnified 150 times
Coloured electron microscope images
Photography:
Oliver Meckes & Nicole Ottawa
www.eyeofscience.com

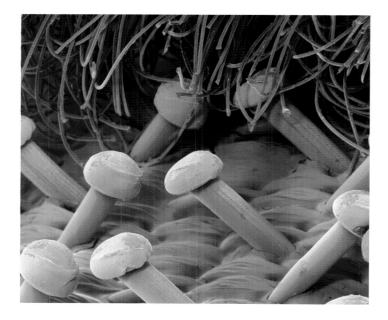

## MICRO AND MACRO

You can also open up new views of things at a microscopic or macroscopic level. How close can I get to the object? How can I show things that the naked eye cannot see? What new visual worlds can I discover and develop in this way? How does the view change if I increase the distance by an enormous amount? Can I combine the two perspectives? What new meanings can objects take on when seen from these perspectives?

Right
**3D Artist:** Niklas Andersson
www.niklasindustries.com

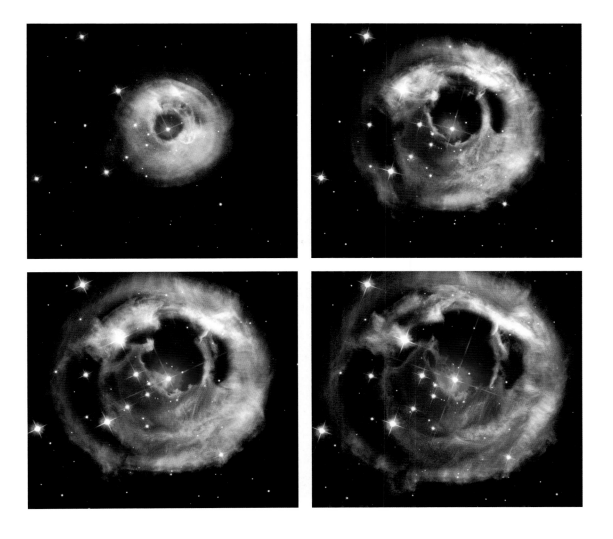

The star V838 Monocerotis is
20,000 light years away from the
Earth. It was photographed in
January 2002 from the Hubble
Space Telescope when, for a short
time, it was 600,000 times brighter
than our sun.
Photography:
NASA, ESA and H.E. Bond (STScI)
http://hubblesite.org

## PROPORTIONS AND DIMENSIONS

Things can often take on surprising
new meanings when you change
their size. What elements can
be reduced or enlarged? What
proportions can be varied? Can you
combine the different dimensions
and proportions? What happens
when dimensions and proportions
are greatly exaggerated?

Above and centre left
Client: Franz Kaldewei
Agency: Brand Factory
Art Direction: Melanie Arnold
Creative Direction: Stefan Böckler
Photography: Uwe Düttmann

Below left
'Kookai – Save the Men'
Client: Kookai
Agency: CLM/BBDO
Art Direction: Pierre-Yves Demarcq
Creative Direction: Anne de Maupeou
Photography: Robert Wyatt

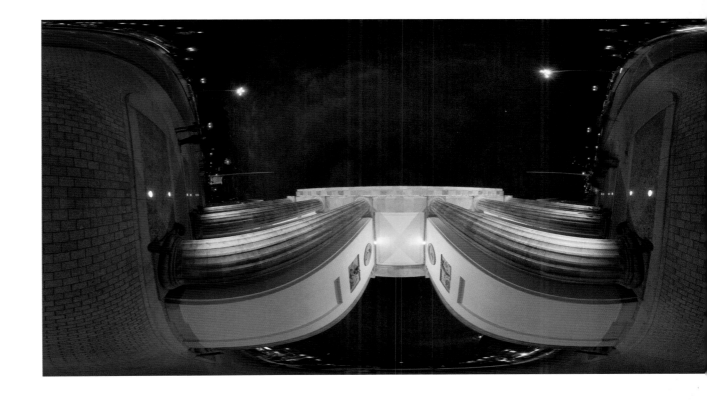

Left
**Band:** Hybrid
**Title:** Wider Angle (Special Edition)
**Project:** CD cover
**Design:** The Design Corporation
www.design4music.com

Below
360° photograph
**Title:** Tata Guines in Havana
**Photography:**
Lukas Maximilian Hüller
www.panvisuals.com

## DISTORTED VIEWS

How can you make the whole object visible at once? Roll it, spread it, unravel it, distort it, flatten it? Can you extend the view by changing the angle? Can you show a succession of movements in a single picture? How can you show a single still picture moving in a film? What can you squash, distort, stretch, or combine in order to broaden the perspective?

Above
**Design:** Syndrome
Micah Hancock, Mars Sandoval,
James Larese
www.syndromestudio.com


Below
**Photography:** Olivo Barbieri
Courtesy of Isabella Brancolini
Arte Contemporanea, Florence

## OBSTRUCTED VIEW

What might disturb or change a view of the real world: haze, fog, broken glasses, short sight, bad circulation, quick movements, a protective shield? How could you deliberately disturb the observer's view – optical illusions, ambiguities, obstacles, refracted light?

Above left
**Illustration:** Charles H. Carver
www.charlescarver.com

Below left
**Photography:** Bill Kouirinis
www.kouirinis.com

## MULTIPLE MEANINGS

Try to imagine possible meanings
when you look closely at an object
or scene. What would you have
to change to alter the meaning?
Colour, form, size, light, surface,
surroundings, people, objects?
What would you have to add in order
to give the situation a new meaning?
What would you have to take away
in order to make the meaning
unusual? What meaning would the
object take on if it were placed in
different surroundings?

Above right
Campaign to save the
Brazilian rainforests.
Client: Fundação S.O.S.
Mata Atlântica
Agency: F/Nazca Saatchi & Saatchi
Photography: João Caetano
Source: Lürzer's Archive 3/2000

Below right
Client: Carlsberg
Agency: VVL/BBDO
Creative Direction: Willy Coppens
Photography: Hans Kroeskamp

Lightweight cross training shoes. *reebok*

Tight safety running shoes *reebok*

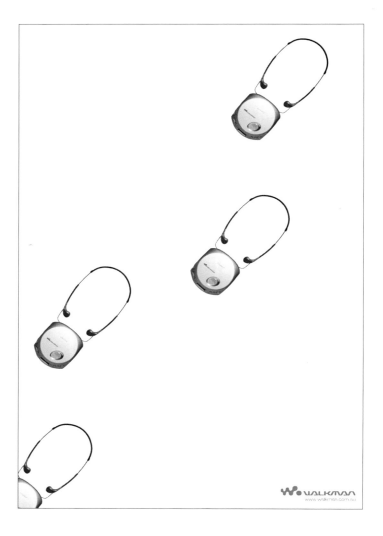

WALKMAN
www.walkman.com.au

## MULTIPLE MEANINGS

Imagine how items could be
rearranged to obtain a surprising
new meaning. How could you
redistribute or reorganize individual
parts to give a different effect? How
should you set up a scene so that it
can take on several meanings? How
could objects be laid out to tell a
complete story? How can you shape,
turn, add or combine objects to
discover something new or
something different in them?

Above
Client: Reebok
Agency: Saatchi & Saatchi
Photography: Ian Butterworth
Source: Lürzer's Archive 4/2002

Left
Client: Sony Australia
Agency: FNL Communications
Art Direction: Mike Miller
Photography: Ian Butterworth

Above right
This scene is based on a classic
optical illusion: if you look at it in
a certain way, you will see a skull.
Client: Christian Dior
Agency: CLM/BBDO
Art Direction: Lèo Berne
Photography: Vincent Peters

Below right
Client: BMW
Agency: GV/Company
Art Direction: Tom Apers
Photography: Wim Vanderwegen

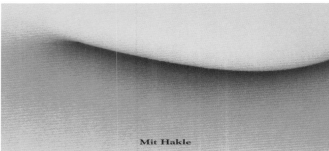

Ohne Hakle

Mit Hakle

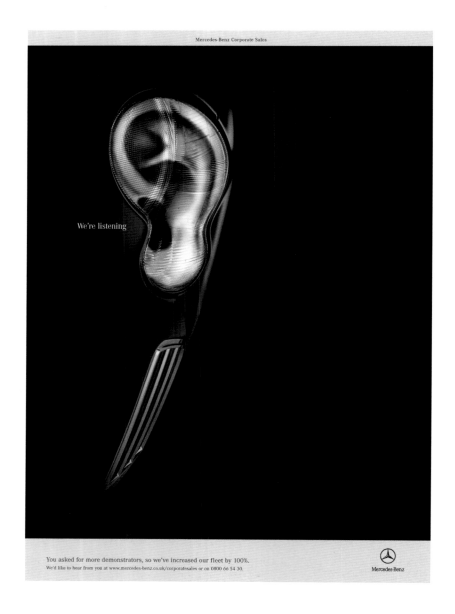

Above left
'Without Hakle' / 'With Hakle'
Client: Hakle toilet tissue
Project: Poster campaign
Agency: Advico Young & Rubicam
Art Direction: Denis Schwarz
Photography: Roland Kroetzier

Below left
Client: Mercedes-Benz
Agency: MBA
Art Direction: Martin Pierson
Photography: Douglas Fisher
Source: Lürzer's Archive 1/2002

## A CHANGE OF MEANING

What can you see that nobody else
has noticed? What might it mean?
What surprising meaning could be
derived from a different perspective?
How could the object be depicted
to take on a double meaning?
How could it be rearranged or
reconstructed in order to give it a
new or different meaning? Could it
take on a new meaning if it was
incorporated into a film sequence?

**Above right**
'Untold horrors lurk on the roads'
Client: Maaf Seguros
Agency: Zapping
Art Direction: Uschi Henkes
Source: Lürzer's Archive 1/2002

**Below right**
Client: Auto Esporte magazine
Agency: Leo Burnett
Art Direction: Daniel Prado
Photography: Danny Yin

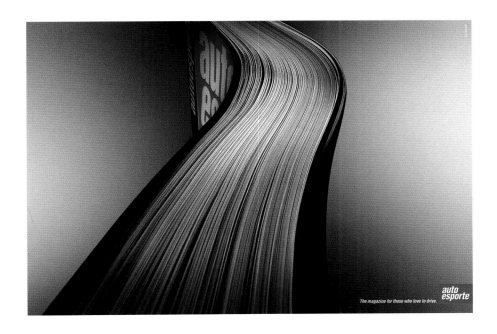

## 2.　What Are Pictures Made Of?

The majority of images we see today are made up of halftone dots or pixels. In other words, practically every picture is assembled from a vast number of tiny individual pieces. It's an interesting exercise to play around with this concept. What, for instance, could you use in place of all these dots to produce pictures? Do they have to be as small as they normally are, or if their size could be varied, what new possibilities would be opened up? If you began to experiment with these parameters, you might for instance use any of the following elements instead of dots or pixels: the compound eyes of insects, the stamens of flowers, light-emitting diodes, or the heads of nails. For the video of *Fell In Love With A Girl* by the White Stripes, the director Michael Gondry used Lego blocks as his basic unit. The whole video was built up with these,

and the movements were stop-motion animated. In fact, almost anything can be used to make a picture. All you need is to find the right relationship between the two parameters of coloured dots and dot-size. Of course, a host of other techniques such as collage are also available, as you will see in the examples that follow.

To avoid being sidetracked into the realms of art, however, we should first of all remind ourselves of our goal. What do we want, what is our basic idea, what is the task that we have to perform? It makes no difference whether you want to create a fictional character, plan a music video, advertise a car or design a fashion catalogue, the question always has to be: what do you want to achieve, and how can you use a particular visual style to reinforce your great idea?

Don't get lost in the world of numbers. Subscribe and get your bearings. **Valor** Financial Newspaper

Client: Valor Financial Newspaper
Agency: Age. Comunicaçoes
Art Direction: Tomás Lorente
Illustration: Tobia Ravá

'Diveo. Wireless Internet for
business. More speed, less
complication.'
Client: Diveo
Agency: TBWA\Cápsula
Comunicação
Art Direction: João Linnue
Illustration: Erevan Chakarain
Source:
Lürzer's Archive 1/2002

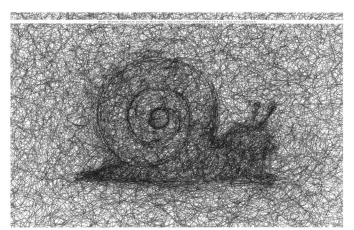 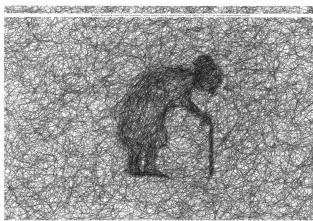

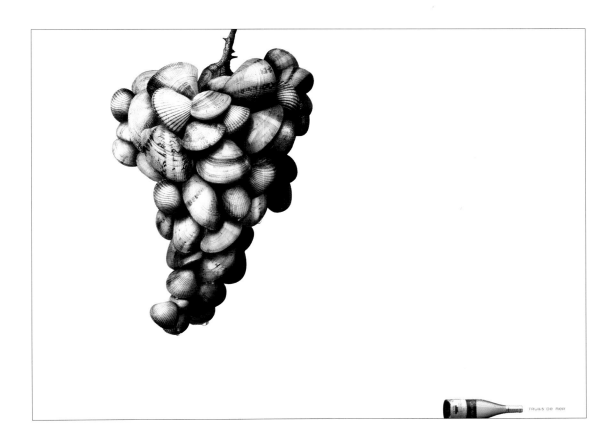

Client: Gonzales Byass
Agency: Bassat Ogilvy
Creative Direction: Jaume Monés
Art Direction: Francesc Talamino
Photography: Joan Garrigosa

Client: Premsons Bazaar
Product: Eternia
Agency: Grey Worldwide
Art Direction: Priti Arora
Creative Direction:
Sanjay Sipahimalani
Photography: Ronnie Wadia

IF YOU LIKE THIS DOLCE & GABBANA SUIT SO MUCH, KEEP STARING AT IT. THAT'S ALL YOU CAN DO NOW THAT RHEA SEN'S BOUGHT IT.

Exclusive designer clothes and accessories for women. From DKNY to D&G. Fendi to Ferre. At Eternia, Premsons Bazaar, Breach Candy. Hurry, they'll be gone in the wink of an eye.    Here today. Gone tomorrow.

ETERNIA

YESTERDAY, THIS WAS THE VERSACE COLLECTION AT ETERNIA, BREACH CANDY. TODAY, IT IS THE SOMAYA COLLECTION AT CITADEL, NAPEAN ROAD.

Exclusive designer clothes and accessories for men and women. From Versace to Valentino. Krizia to Kenzo. Now at Eternia, Premsons Bazaar, Breach Candy. Tomorrow, they could all be gone.    Here today. Gone tomorrow.

ETERNIA

## VISUAL BUILDING BLOCKS

What objects or materials have never been used to make pictures: telephone wires, fingertips, planets, fizzy drinks, mathematical formulae, mouse noses? What patterns, colours, fabrics could be used for pictures? How could you make pictures without using dots, lines or collages? What would images look like if they were made from gas, chemical reactions, or liquids? Could you combine these with ordinary images?

Above right
Client: Voimariini
Agency: Sek Grey
Art Direction: Arto Komulainen
Photography: Carl Warner
www.carlwarner.com

Below right
Client: Sunderland NHS Trust
Agency: Different Ltd
Art Direction: Ian Millen
Photography: Chris Auld

Left
Client: vasakronan.se
Agency: Schumacher, Jersild,
Wessman & Enander
Art Direction: Marita Kuntonen
Photography: Hans Gedda
Source: Lürzer's Archive 1/2000

This commercial for Vodaphone is made entirely from text. The leading man, the buildings, and the city through which he moves are constructed from words or combinations of letters. The meaning and the actions are reinforced by sound effects and dialogue.

## MORE BUILDING BLOCKS

Imagine what people or other living creatures might be made of: ten thousand tiny hands, string, door handles. How could you create pictures from forms of energy or other phenomena that are usually invisible: sound waves, the Northern Lights, lightning, breath? Would it be possible to create pictures out of the component parts of a product?

Above right
Client: Vodaphone/France Telecom
Agency: BMP DDB Ltd
Art Direction: Paul Angus
Post-Production:
Partizan Midi Minuit
Director: Antoine Bardou-Jaquet

Below, left and right
Client: Mars
Agency: BBDO Düsseldorf
Creative Direction: Marco Pupella
Art Direction: Katja Luckas
Photography: Jost Hiller

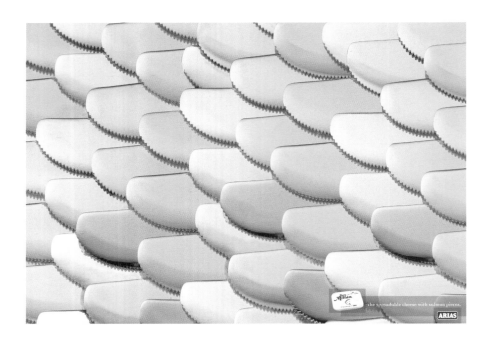

Left
'The spreadable cheese
with salmon pieces'
Client: Arias
Agency: Tandem DDB
Art Direction:
Pablo Rodriguez de Miguel
Photography: Santiago Boil
Source: Lürzer's Archive 4/2002

## MORE BUILDING BLOCKS

What articles or objects can be
combined to make pictures? How
could you put them together to
produce a meaningful image? What
has never been used before to make
a collage? How could a collage be
used in a film, and what would it
look like? How and from what could
a 3D collage be made?

CUT FOR YOU.

Right and below left
Client: Levi Strauss & Co
Agency: neogama/BBH
Art Direction: Marcio Ribas
Creative Direction:
Alexandre Gama
Photography: Bruno Cals

# 3.    Playing With Layers

If you're looking for ways of deriving new meanings from reality, or discovering surprising visual ideas in it, a fruitful strategy can be to play around with different layers or levels. The basic pattern is easy to grasp. Combine elements taken from the picture's background with others from the foreground. You can do this in several different ways: for instance, through a particular perspective you can get objects to overlap, either supplementing each other or apparently merging together so that they form an original or surprising combination. Another variation is to add objects onto a picture afterwards, or to superimpose pictures so that between them they produce new meanings. As you will see from the examples that follow, the possible range of creative solutions is enormous, and in all probability the best ideas have not yet been discovered. This type of visual effect is relatively rare, especially in the field of moving images. You might perhaps try to use these techniques for the opening credits of a film, with quite stunning results: imagine focusing initially on something specific, and then the camera pans to a totally different picture that confronts the audience with a totally different meaning. If you let your thinking wander in these directions, you will automatically enter the realm of visual ambiguity, much as we see it in optical illusions such as the works of M. C. Escher.

## FIGURE AND BACKGROUND

Can you imagine combining two
independent items so that together
they form a third, completely new
object? What can you superimpose,
move behind, or add on in order to
produce a new meaning or a new
perspective? How can you use
something transparent in order
to bring objects together?

Right
'Doesn't hurt at all!' Campaign
for low-cost health insurance
Client: Hang Seng Bank
Agency: J. Walter Thompson
Art Direction: Eugene Tsoh
Photography: Raymond Chau
Source: Lürzer's Archive 5/2002

## LAYERS OF SPACE

How can you use spatial depth in order to combine objects or scenes? How can scenes be linked together in three-dimensional space? How can the eyes be deceived by an object in the background overlapping with an object in the foreground?

Above
Client: Air France
Agency: Euro RSCG BETC
Director: Michel Gondry
Post-Production: Buf
Production: Partizan
www.partizan.com

Below, left and right
Client: Levi Strauss & Co
Agency: Bartle Bogle Hegarty
Art Direction: Alex Lim
Creative Direction:
Marthinus Strydom
Photography: Nadav Kander

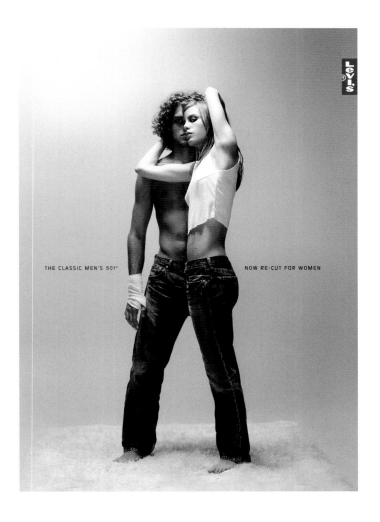

Schauspielhaus

S

Marco Polo Wunderwelt
14.1.- 23.2.2003 / 20:00 Uhr

Client: Schauspielhaus Wien
(Vienna theatre company)
Agency: Jung von Matt/Donau
Art Direction: Günter Eder
Photography: Dieter Brasch
Artwork: Viennapaint

Computer Game Trailer: XIII
Publisher: Ubi Soft
Developer: Ubi Soft
© 2002 Ubi Soft Entertainment.
All Rights Reserved.

Left and below
Client: Perrier
Agency: Ogilvy & Mather
Art Direction: Thierry Chiumino
Photography: Vincent Dixon
Source:
Lürzer's Archive 5/2002

Above right
Client: McIlhenny Co. Tabasco
Agency: DDB
Art Direction: Matt Spett
Photography: Phillip Esparza
Illustration: Image Tap
Source: Lürzer's Archive 3/2002


Below right
Client: Coca-Cola
Agency: McCann-Erickson
Art Direction: Rebeca Díaz
Creative Direction: Juan Nonzioli
Photography: Sara Zorraquino

## STORIES IN LAYERS

How can you produce humour by superimposing different layers? How can you develop a witty scene or narrate a story? How can you link different visual layers together so that they combine to form a single punchline?

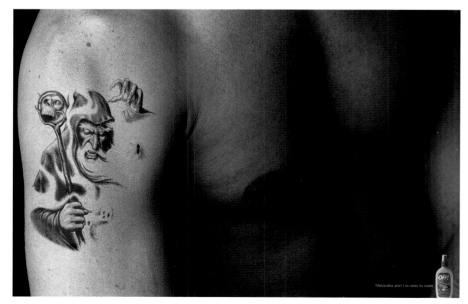

Above left
Client: DaimlerChrysler Co
Agency: BBDO Korea
Art Direction: Choi-hee Kang
Creative Direction: Dong-su Yi

Centre and below left
'Mosquitos aren't so easy to scare.'
Client: S. C. Johnson
Agency: Giovanni, FCB
Art Direction: Marcus Adriano
Photography: Aderi Costa
Source: Lürzer's Archive 4/2002

## CLICHÉS

How can you play with different layers so that you automatically get rid of clichés and hackneyed associations? How can you give a new meaning to one part of an image by drawing attention to it? How can a scene take on a new meaning by merging something from the background with other visual elements?

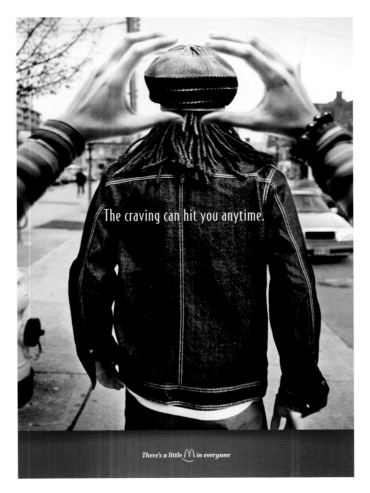

Client: McDonald's
Source: Lürzer's Archive

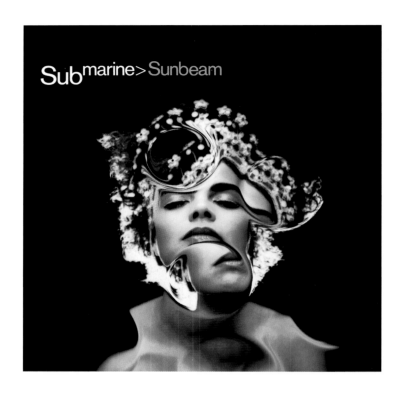

## SPACE IN DIFFERENT MEDIA

How can you open up an unusual perspective by juggling with visual or spatial layers? What can be superimposed on what? What things or images can be superimposed in order to produce a new image? How can you combine spatial perspectives? Or how can you combine features of the medium with specific elements of the picture? How might they influence each other?

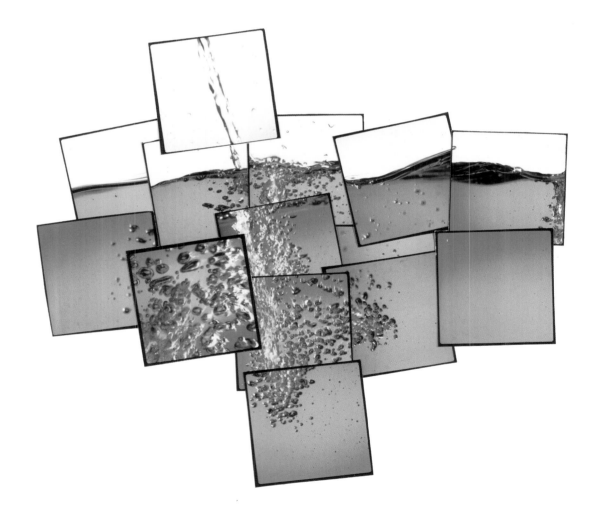

Above left
Artist: Submarine
Title: Sunbeam
Project: CD cover
Design: The Design Corporation
www.design4music.com
Photography: Ian Brodie

Below left
Photography: Michael Rathmayer

Above left
**Client:** Oslo Piercing Studio
**Agency:** Leo Burnett
**Art Direction:** Erik Heisholt,
Marianne Arnesen


Below left
**Client:** Ek-Chai Distribution System
**Agency:** Ogilvy & Mather
**Art Direction:** Vasan Wangpaitoon
**Creative Direction:** Nikorm Kulkosa

## LAYERS IN DIFFERENT MEDIA

How can you produce layered
images: projections, painting,
collages, montages? How can
visual layers be accumulated,
superimposed, lined up, assembled?
How could an object take on a new
meaning by being combined with
something else, inserted elsewhere,
or copied into another image?

*Steven*

stevemadden.com

SHOES BY STEVE MADDEN

Above right
Client: Steve Madden
Art Direction: Tom Kane
Photography: Eva Mueller
www.evamueller.com

Below right
Campaign for a hair salon
Client: Shampoo Planet
Agency: KesselsKramer
Art Direction: Yugi Tokuda
Photography: Bart Oomes
Source: Lürzer's Archive 4/2002

Cut by Shampoo Planet

Cut by Shampoo Planet

# 4.  When Graphics Meet Images

In this department of our visual lab, you are invited to discover new ways to create a productive relationship between text or graphic elements and images or film sequences. Of course this subject is obviously too vast to be encompassed by just a few pages, but all the same I'm sure you will find a few interesting and fertile ideas here to improve your visual thinking. Basically, the trick is to bring together two things that normally have very little in common. Graphic design all too often does nothing but add to the aesthetic appeal of a picture without actively reinforcing its message. The question therefore arises of how graphic design and photography can be combined into an indivisible, symbiotic unit in which the two elements merge and complement each other. How can graphic design be made an integral part of the picture's central theme? How might you think about images in a photo or film shoot in such a way that they could only be completed through the later addition of graphic elements? Ad industry creatives might find suitable inspiration for this in the spheres of motion graphics and broadcast design.

How could you incorporate typography so that it too becomes an integral part of the concept and forms an organic whole with the image? It doesn't matter what experiments you are interested in or what goal you are pursuing, this is another area in which it will be worth your while to work on these inner visual worlds. While you are testing the ground, it may also be helpful to do some sketching and doodling, so that you can get a feel for how your ideas will look and which of them will work best.

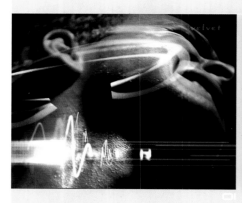 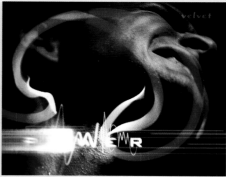 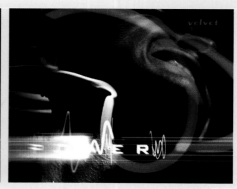

Client: Sky Sports
Art Direction: Barry Bichard
Director and Designer:
Matthias Zentner
Post-Production:
velvet mediendesign
www.velvet.de

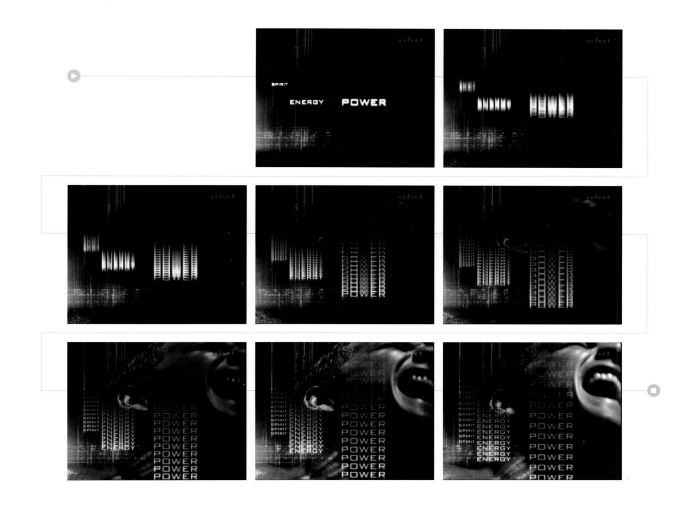

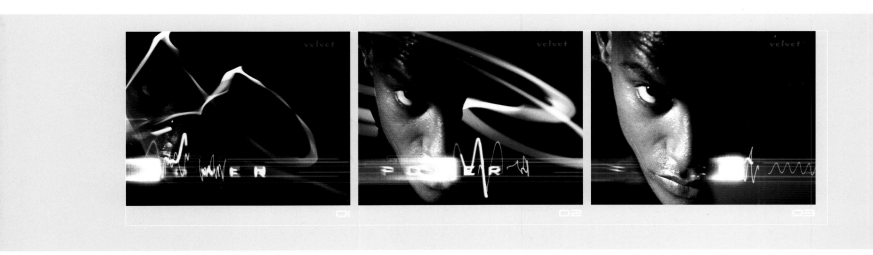

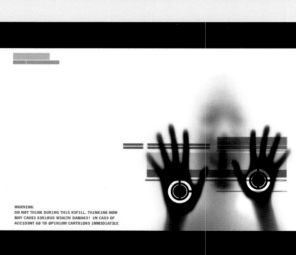

Above
Ident for the German
TV channel Pro Sieben
Campaign: XXL
Creative Direction: Barbara Simon

Below, left and right
Client: Suk&Koch
Directors, Producers, Sound,
Music, Design: Suk&Koch
Actor: Kim Min
www.sukkoch.com

## TYPOGRAPHIC TRICKS

Where within the image can the typography be placed? Can words and letters be a part of the image? Can typography become a living creature that can move around inside the image? Can written signs emerge from the image itself: labels, road signs, neon signs, posters, advertisements on public transport? Could you place scenes side by side to produce a text in a kind of collage? Can you integrate signs, signals, symbols in a picture to reinforce the message of the text? Could you turn convention on its head, using typography that fills the picture, and putting nothing but tiny images in the foreground?

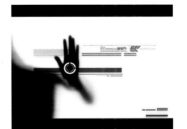

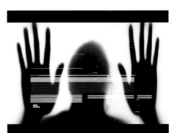

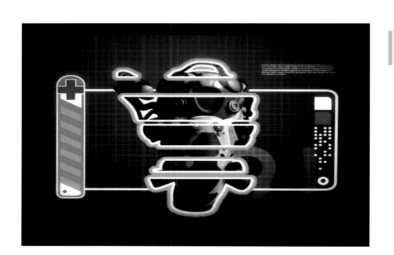

### GRAPHICS AND 3D ANIMATION

How can graphic design or typography be used to enhance or expand 3D animated pictures or films? In what exciting ways can they be combined to create new visual styles? How could 2D graphics reinforce the message of 3D animation, or raise it to a higher level?

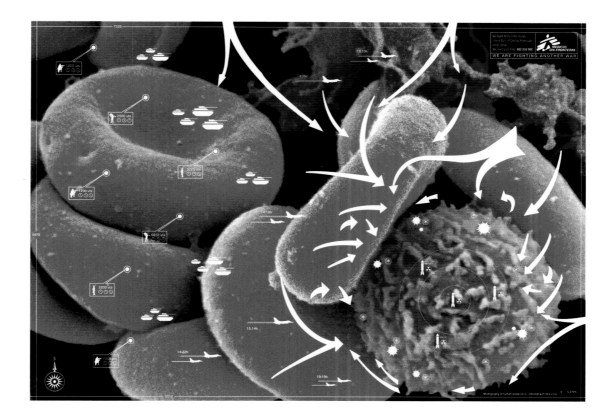

Left and below
Design: Syndrome Studio
Micah Hancock

Right
'We are fighting another war'
Campaign for a charity supplying
medical aid to war-torn regions.
Client: Médicins Sans Frontières
Agency: McCann-Erickson
Creative Direction:
Nicolas Hollander
Art Direction: Vanessa Sanz
Photography: Getty Images

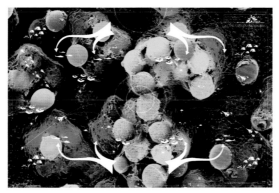
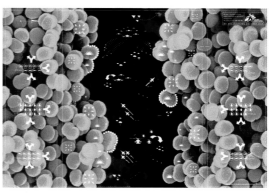

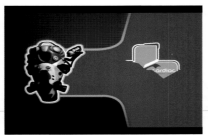

session one:

cropped sweater by: **ILLIG**
resurrected camo pants by: **TAG RAG**
boots: **MODEL'S OWN BOOTS**
vintage tech bracelet: **NO REPLY**
gun by: **SYNDROME**

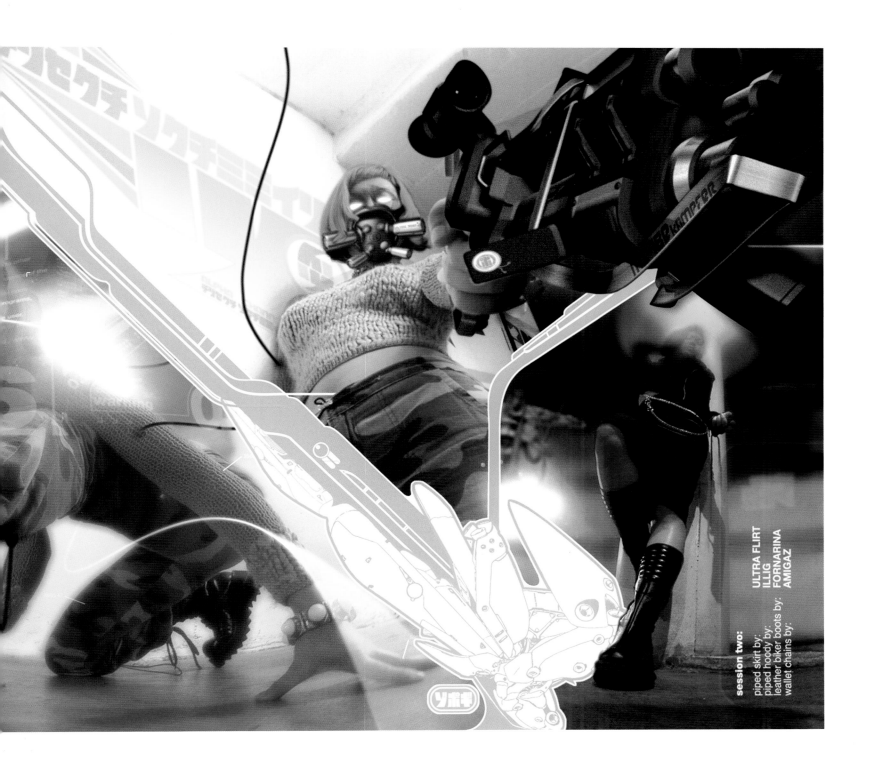

session two:

piped skirt by: **ULTRA FLIRT**
piped hoody by: **ILLIG**
leather biker boots by: **FORNARINA**
wallet chains by: **AMIGAZ**

Design: Syndrome Studio
Micah Hancock, Mars Sandoval
www.syndromestudio.com

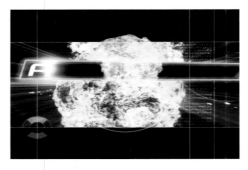
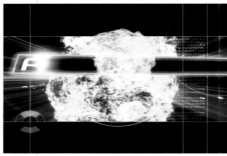

Movie Central ident –
'Adrenaline Drive'
Client: Corus Entertainment
Post-Production: Spin Toronto
Director: Nicholas Kadima
Designer: Steven Lewis

## COMBINING PARTS

How could a 2D graphic move around in a 3D space? How could graphics incorporate a 3D space in which actions take place? How could graphic design become a surface onto which images could be projected? How could images be combined with graphic design: side by side, intermingled, superimposed, collaged? Could part of a picture be replaced by graphic elements, or vice versa?

Above right
Client: Comedy Central
Production: Eyeball NYC
Creative Direction: Limore Shur
Art Direction: Julian Bevan
Animation: Sal Midolo
Illustration: Andrew Wendel

Below right
Client: FHRC, Sony Europe
Designer: Alex Rutterford
Producer: Christian Hogue
Lost In Space
Photography: James Cant
www.lostinspace.com

MORE COMBINATIONS

How can typography take on additional functions within a picture? What could be hidden in a written character and revealed when it is twisted, turned or opened up? What has never been done before with written signs? In what new ways could 2D design be integrated into pictures? What has never been tried?

Above
Computer Game Trailer: XIII
Publisher: Ubi Soft
Developer: Ubi Soft
© 2002 Ubi Soft Entertainment.
All Rights Reserved.

Left
Book Design: Florian Scharinger
With the cooperation of
Getty Images.

Right
Client: Adidas
Agency: 180 Communication
Art Direction: Laen Sanches
Photography: Darren Regnier
Source: Lürzer's Archive 6/2001

# 5.  Expanding Reality

What would you like to add to reality, what could be extended, what could be left out? Combining the real with the fictional means taking a first step into an absolutely limitless field of creative possibilities. In this context it can be useful to experiment with two of the ways of seeing that were outlined in Part 2 of this book: controlling images and dreaming with your eyes open. For instance, look at the scene around you and add elements drawn from your imagination, or close your eyes, recall images from your memory bank, and add fictional elements to them. Whatever you do, the basic idea is the same: you use these mental tools quite deliberately in order to train the muscles of your imagination and to give yourself a greater degree of freedom.

If you are in search of a solution to a specific problem, the pages that follow will present you with a wide playing field. Do not, however, let the examples limit you, for there are countless more ideas out there, just waiting for you to discover them. Make a game out of juggling, combining, varying, shifting, twisting the visual elements and the fragments of ideas as they flow before your mind's eye. Take the picture apart, and then experiment with all its sections. How much can be changed: a few pixels, a whole object, or everything except a single detail? What could be replaced by something else, by something artificial? What can be added to an image of the real world: an artistic style, different materials, animation, still images, puppets? Give an animated character the arms of a real person, or take a real object like a car and give it hand-drawn wheels. You can even conceal your variations so cleverly that people will only notice them if they take a second look. You can also switch between reality and fantasy: insert real images into illustrations, 3D animations or other picture styles. Switch between worlds – evenly, jerkily, step by step, or imperceptibly. Construct things in your mind's eye that you have never seen in real life. You have a licence to do anything that is new, surprising, and against all the conventions.

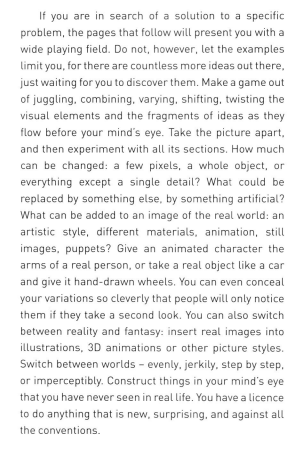

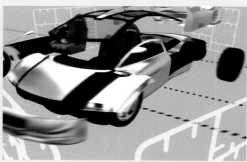

Right
Client: McDonald's
Project: TV ad
Agency: DDB Chicago
Production: Eyeball NYC
Creative Direction: Limore Shur

  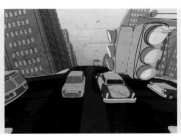

Left
This ident for a TV channel devoted to DIY shows a man with a model kit for a toy car. He throws the pieces in front of him, the car puts itself together, he gets in and drives away.
Client: DIY Network
Project: Channel ident
Production: Viewpoint Studios
Creative Direction: Jeff Sears
Producer: Adrienne Gum

## REALITY AND FICTION

How can pictures be combined
with animation, illustration
and other visual styles? Where
and how can reality and the
imaginary world supplement
each other? Can only sections be
replaced or can the whole picture
be transformed piece by piece
into something new? How can
animation be made to look like
reality, and how can reality be
copied artificially?

Left and above
Client: Toyota
Agency: Saatchi & Saatchi
Art Direction: Kathryn Nassr
Production: Industry Films
Animation: Red Rover Studios

Right
The look of an illustration was
created by superimposing a real
car on a painted studio set.
Client: DaimlerChrysler AG
Photography: Dietmar Henneka
Set Construction: Peter Boeck
www.henneka.com

Below, left and right
Client: Sony
Agency: Saatchi & Saatchi
Art Direction: Andrew Clarke
Photography: Gina Garan
Source: Lürzer's Archive 6/2001

Above, left and right
Client: Steve Madden
Project: Magazine and TV ads
Agency: Hampel Stefanides
Art Direction: Tom Kane
Illustration/Photography:
Butch Belair
Post-Production: Curious Pictures

## STAGED REALITY 1

What can be added to reality to
create a fictional image: toys,
dummies, dolls of all kinds, stage
sets, backdrops, painted scenery,
superimpositions, projections?
How could you make real-life
versions of illustrations, cartoons
or fictional characters and
include them in images?

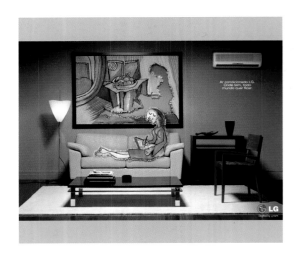 

## STAGED REALITY 2

Where could real images, or parts of
them, be inserted: into other images,
different visual styles, illustrations,
paintings, silent movies, flipbooks,
old documents or posters? How
could you insert artificial elements
or fictional characters into real
images so that they can no longer
be recognized as unreal?

Above left
'LG air conditioning. Wherever
it is, everyone wants to stay.'
Client: LG Electronics
Agency: Código
Art Direction: Augusto Canani
Photography: Celso Chittolina
Illustration: Jorge Gariba
Source: Lürzer's Archive 2/2002

Below left
Client: Canal+
Agency: Contrapunto
Art Direction: Javier Furones
Creative Direction: Antonio Montero
Photography: Ivá Manzanero

Right
This ad shows robots testing
the special abilities of a new
Adidas sports shoe. Computer
animation was integrated with
live-action film.
Client: Adidas
Agency: TBWA\Chiat
Creative Direction: Chuck McBride
Art Direction: Todd Grant
Director: David Fincher
Post-Production: Digital Domain

Client: Francesco Biasia
Agency: D'Adda, Lorenzini,
Vigorelli, BBDO
Art Direction: Gian Pietro Vigorelli
Photography: Ilan Rubin

On what levels can reality be manipulated by fiction: establishing connections, expanding or distorting objects, disturbing or interfering with the conventional and familiar, breaking up elements or scenes? What happens when a vital component of reality is replaced by an artificial one? Why might a real image be transformed?

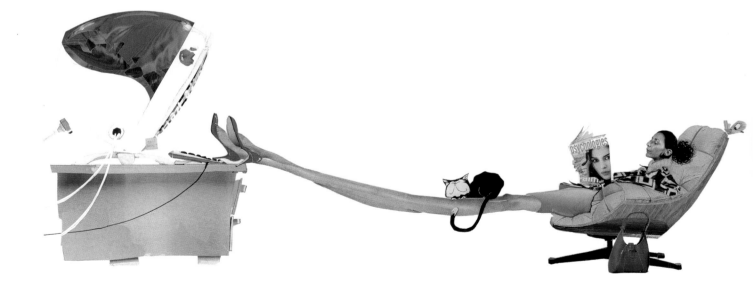

Above right
Client: Galliano
Source: Lürzer's Archive

Below right
Illustration: Robert Wagt
'Stress' for *Psychologies* magazine

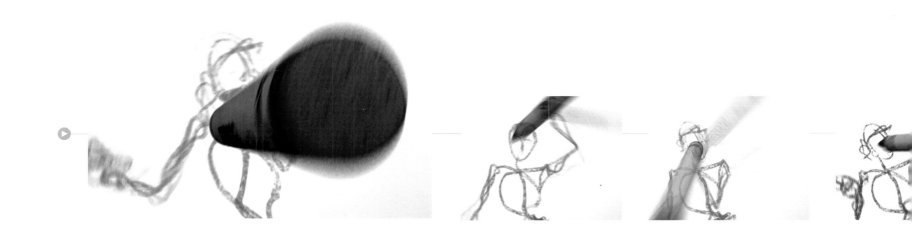

Left
Client: IDA – The Society
of Danish Engineers
Agency: Sylvesterhvid & Partners
Art Direction: Morten Even
Photography and Concept:
Jeppe Gudmundsen-Holmgreen
www.jeppegudmundsen.com
Repro: www.schillerdigital.dk

In this TV ad, a doodle grabs hold of a crayon and begins to draw itself. Bit by bit it changes its face and body, adding more details and improvements.

## MANIPULATING REALITY

How can a real image be manipulated, or what can it be combined with: mechanical influences, film processing and manipulation, collages made from different materials, rearrangement of its parts, introduction of unfamiliar elements?

Above
Client: AT&T
Agency: Wunderman
Creatives: Jules Filicia, Leigh-Anne Wiester, Wayne Schombs
Production: Fred Slobodin
Post-Production: Quiet Man

Right
Client: Campaign Brief Asia
Product: Specialist magazine for the ad industry
Agency: Saatchi & Saatchi
Art Direction: Maurice Wee
Photography: Stanley Wong
Source: Lürzer's Archive 1/2002

## 6.   Morphing and Shape-Shifting

Below
Client: Kia Motor Corp.
Post-Production: Colorado FX
www.coloradofx.com

A fluent transition from one image to another, and objects changing into other objects – these concepts are now commonplace in films, cartoons, games and commercials. Viewers have become so accustomed to morphing and shape-shifting that no one bats an eyelid any more. The formula here, as elsewhere, is that you will only grab attention by deviating from the norm. The question therefore arises as to what areas of visual space have not yet been explored by the morphers and shape-shifters. What new territories are waiting to be discovered? You should therefore begin by asking not what is possible, but what would be amazing and original. Try to forget what you have already seen, and free yourself from your own technical knowledge. For instance, most people think morphs should be as elegant and smooth as possible, but you could try the opposite. Make them flicker, jerk, stumble, or insert intermediate images.

The public has got used to morphing, and so let us ask the following question: what could you add to a changing picture in order to load it with more meaning? What would the effect be, for instance, if a 3D image changed into a 2D one? Or supposing the process was helped along by some sort of apparatus, or by a lot of tiny creatures? It might not be a figure or an object that changes but the whole setting. Things could appear at different stages of completion, and then rearrange themselves in different places. We could observe the process on the level of single atoms, or in musical rhythms. Morphing and shape-shifting can also be regarded as a special form of editing. How can one image be made to change into another? What has never been tried? Once again, the best testing-ground is your own imagination. During the 'concept' phase, there are no limits to what you can try in your search for the best solution to your problem. But in your quest, don't just stick with the first decent idea that comes along – develop as many as possible, to give yourself a pool of ideas from which you can select the best one. It's a little like a lottery, because the more tickets you have, the greater your chances of winning.

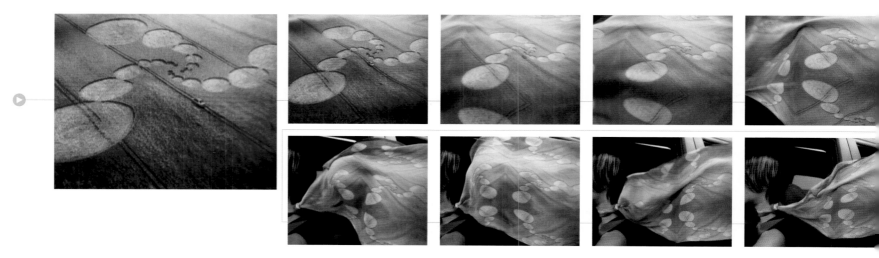

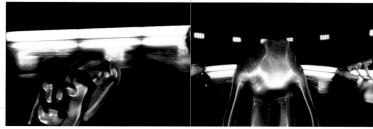

Right
Artist: Louise
Song: Beautiful Inside
Project: Music video
Special Effects: Glassworks Ltd
Creative Direction: Stephen Butler

## CHANGES AND TRANSITIONS

Morphing can go through several
stages: a figure might, for instance,
go through eight different phases
before it reaches its final form, or
there might be one intermediate
phase in which another face
emerges. Would it be possible to
manipulate the image itself during
a morphing sequence? The scene
could be coloured or black and
white, the image could fall apart and
then reassemble itself, the edges
could begin to blur, or could change
in other ways. Could a real person
change into a fictional one? How
would such a transformation look
from the inside – the bones, the
heart, the brain, the soul? Might an
artificial being have the quality that
it is in a constant state of change?

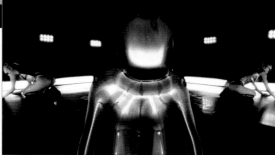

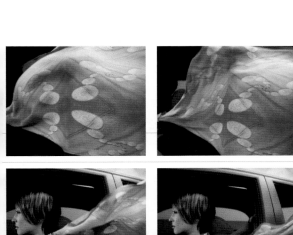

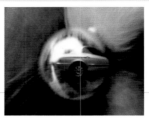

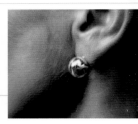

## THE SOUND OF MORPHING

What sounds have never been used in morphing? What would be new and original? If an object changes into something else, what would the transition sound like? Could the transformation be linked to the rhythms of the surrounding world – heartbeats, music, breathing, day and night, background noises, gasps of fear, drops of sweat?

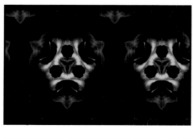
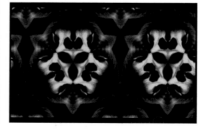
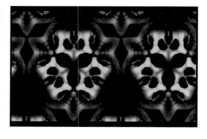

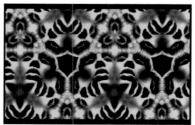

Above
**Client:** Kia Motor Corp.
**Post-Production:** Colorado FX

Left
**Client:** Channel Nine
**Production:** velvet mediendesign
**Post-Production:** Das Werk GmbH
**Director:** Matthias Zentner
www.velvet.de

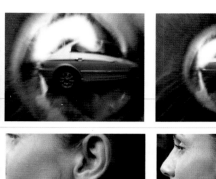

Right
Client: Marithé François Girbaud
Agency: Air
Art Direction: Dimitri Smilenko
Creative Direction: Tho Van Tran
Photography: Geoffroy de Boismenu
www.geoffroydeboismenu.com

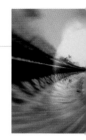

## THE SPEED OF CHANGE

What would the effect be if the
change were gradual, extending
throughout the duration of the film,
like the ageing process? How would
it be if it remained static for a while
during an intermediate phase? Could
a change be shown in slow motion,
or over a period of a thousand years?
What has no one ever seen before?
What would be striking and original?

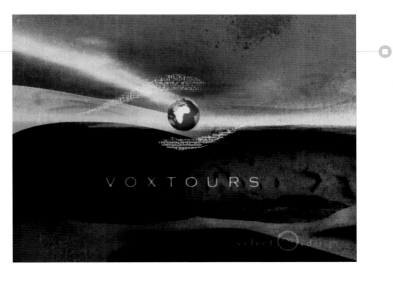

Above and right
Client: Voxtours
Post-Production and Production:
velvet mediendesign
Director: Matthias Zentner
www.velvet.de

Below
Client: Charlotte USA
Title: Life In Balance
Agency: Luquire George Andrews
Post-Production: Spin Atlanta
Designer: Keith Adams

Client: Saturn
Agency: London Project/redblue Marketing
Post-Production and Production:
velvet mediendesign, www.velvet.de
Director: Matthias Zentner

# 7. Worlds Without Frontiers

Since time immemorial, technological developments have been accompanied by the maxim that whatever is technically possible will be used. This is particularly true of image-producing technology, because the public is constantly clamouring for new images, narrative devices, and visual stimuli. Since computers have virtually no limitations, it's often only the budgets and media involved that impose restrictions. Let us imagine, though, that in the near future there will be networked supermedia with biological interfaces that can accomplish anything. What sort of things do you think you might see on your screen, and what might you use them for? Would they be special effects spectaculars, stories wrapped in visual symphonies that give the viewer the biggest possible emotional kick? The idea is not so way out when you realize that children today are already free to select the level of consciousness they wish to act on. Computer games and similar devices can deliver an emotional kick through acoustic, visual or kinaesthetic elements that will create whatever state is required. Imagine what it would be like if all the codes of the brain had been deciphered, so that every emotion could be deliberately triggered by way of targeted stimuli. What would we use the media for, and what would they make us see, feel, hear?

It always surprises me that the creatives of today seem to have no idea what new visual languages or other forms of expression will be entering our heads in future through the media. During my training courses, I find that even professionals from the advertising and media worlds have difficulty grasping the liberating idea that everything is possible. They cling to clichés and reproduce endless modifications of images that they have already seen somewhere at some time. The fact that new visual worlds and new ways of telling stories are already with us is demonstrated most clearly by the film industry. The speed of storytelling has become breathtaking. Until the mid-1960s, there was a standard narrative technique that would move from wide shots into the relevant setting and thus give the viewer an overall orientation. Only then would the eye be directed towards the details of the scene. Today, hardly anyone bothers with this kind of introductory sequence, because audiences now seem to have learned to complete the most complex of scenes in their heads automatically, and so they no longer require this kind of visual aid. The result has been a tightening-up of the narrative style. Research has shown that the younger generation is able to select information far more quickly than older generations – trained by computer games, music videos and the Internet, this mental process has spawned these new forms of narrative technique.

Nowadays, the fields of advertising, films and computer games are forever seeking new ways to show scenes and concepts that are invisible, against the laws of nature, or that simply don't exist in the real world. Invisible things might include blood circulation, radiation, washing powder dissolving the dirt in a fabric, or alien forms of sensory perception. Creatives and designers must therefore try to visualize things that nobody has ever seen, and so of course they cannot and should not try to base their visions on the familiar, since the public will never accept them as new or original. On the other hand, however, the idea cannot be too alien, or we will be unable to find a point of identification and so the newness will seem valueless. A client of an advertising agency summed up the problem very neatly: 'Is that supposed to be new? I've never seen anything like it!' Or, in the reputed words of Woody Allen: 'The best ideas are fifteen minutes ahead of their time. Ideas that are light years ahead are simply ignored.' In any event, you need a degree of courage to commit yourself to new visual and narrative techniques. However, your courage will often be rewarded – with the attention of the target group, prizes from the judges, and a big leap ahead of the competition. And so in this department of our visual lab, I invite you to enter new territory from which clichés have been banned and in which you can see objects and scenery that no one has ever seen before.

## What can you see?

Most of the time we only see what we know. When an architect walks through a city, he or she sees different things from those that you might notice – the composition of materials, architectural devices, how the façades are put together, the stylistic features. You and I, meanwhile, may only see one house among many. If you want to create new ideas and new worlds, it's invaluable to acquire a wide spectrum of knowledge and to open yourself up to areas of life that you know nothing about.

How might an animal or a mythical monster perceive its environment? How can you convey to a viewer that he or she is now looking at the world through this creature's eyes? Knowledge becomes a springboard for the imagination if you know, for instance, that bats 'see' by means of ultrasonic echo-location, and beetles, birds and many types of fish find their way by means of the earth's magnetic field. Bees navigate by detecting the plane of polarization of daylight, and the rattlesnake has a heat-sensitive pit in front of its eye that gives it a kind of three-dimensional infra-red picture. Many animals can register vibrations that escape even the most modern measuring devices, and a dog's nose is said to be a million times more sensitive than a human's. Let your imagination get to work on these snippets of information, and picture in your mind's eye how these creatures' faculties work. How could they be visualized? How could you get an audience to actually see such extraordinary forms of perception? There is nothing stupid about this kind of speculation; it's simply a means of expanding your visual repertoire so that you can be open to new ideas.

What else would you like to visualize? Maybe a bird's-eye view of how people move or behave in a large crowd? Or even whole nations moving over the Earth throughout a period of time, or groups of people forming a single organic body that functions according to precise laws? The more unusual the concept, the more useful it will be to deepen your knowledge of scientific research. For example, you might find some stimulating ideas in the so-called 'morphic fields' described by the English biologist Rupert Sheldrake. He maintains that all the invisible ties between man and animal and those between animals themselves – such as insect communities – depend on a kind of invisible 'field'. He uses this theory to explain how individual creatures that live in communities – flocks of birds, shoals of fish – coordinate their movements as if they were guided by an invisible hand. How could this field be depicted, and how can individuals change into an organically growing, moving collective body?

Set your imagination free, and remember that reality begins with a dream. That is why your imagination and your ability to conjure up clear images are the treasure chest that must accompany you on your journey to unknown lands. But do not under any circumstances begin by asking what course you should plot. You are free to indulge in whatever fantasies you like. I often find myself criticizing the advertising and entertainment industries because of their lack of imagination and their adherence to visual clichés that have lost their impact to the point of sheer senselessness. And so turn your gaze inward, onto the movie screen in your mind, and visualize images and scenes that you have always wanted to see. Of course you can choose scenes from films or adverts that already exist, but change them according to your own predilections.

Let us say we are planning one of those all-action blockbuster movies in which a car explodes, how would we depict it? My question would be: What have we never seen before? In view of the laws of nature, what would be impossible for us to show? The search for creative answers could lead to all kinds of interesting ideas. What are the chemical and physical processes that take place during an explosion, and have you ever wondered how they could be pictured? What would they look like if seen from the inside (for example, from inside the car), and what would be the effects of the outward movement from this perspective? Have you ever visualized an explosion in terms of the sound waves, the pressure, the heat (if these aspects could be seen separately), or in terms of its outward movement at different speeds? What effects might you achieve by filming such an explosion with a thermal camera, or by showing it from multiple angles? You might show a succession of views from the perspective of different people and objects affected. Here is another suggestion: supposing you had a slow-motion camera that moved with the outermost shock waves, showing what happened to the objects that were hit? If you give yourself time to play around with ideas like this, you will discover an astonishing array of exciting possibilities. Supposing the camera passed from the expanding outer regions of the explosion through to its epicentre? And what if, as the camera moved, we looked out again at what was happening beyond the explosion, perhaps as if seeing it through a distorting mirror? Have you ever seen an explosion that moved to the rhythm of the musical soundtrack, or have you seen one viewed from below?

These innovations could be fun for the creative and, especially, fun for the public. Mind Matrix 1 and Mind Matrix 2 on the following pages will provide you with a playground for games like these, and enable you to develop completely new and original visual ideas and scenes. The headings and questions are meant to serve as stimuli, and should very quickly take you into previously uncharted territory.

## The Mind-Matrix 1

The questions in Mind Matrix 1 will offer you a number of useful stimuli in fourteen different areas of visual thinking. It's easy to use: just pick any question, and apply it to whatever task or project you're working on.

If, for instance, you are planning an ad to show that a new mid-range BMW accelerates faster than its competitors, you might choose the category 'Taking Pictures Apart'. Visualize the car moving, and then split the image up into its component parts: driver, dashboard, chassis, road, tyres, surroundings. Maybe start with the driver, and ask yourself how you can show the lightning acceleration through him – facial expressions, distortion as in a rocket launch, hair streaming backwards, head pressed against the headrest, white-knuckled hands as he grips the steering wheel, and so on.

Go through every pictorial element in turn, and collect your ideas. Each of the fourteen categories will help you to immerse yourself in different visual aspects of your project and therefore to come up with original angles. Don't restrict yourself to a single question for each category; instead, try to come up with several, and combine them. Let's continue with our BMW project. See if you could use unusual perspectives to show the driver reacting to the acceleration. Perhaps you can have different speeds running parallel through the picture – with the driver and car moving at normal speed, and the landscape in slow motion.

By combining the questions in the fourteen categories, you could come up with an almost infinite set of variations. If you are looking for ideas related to computer animation, film, computer games, or advertising, you can apply the questions in Mind Matrix 1 to the key terms of Mind Matrix 2. These terms refer mainly to qualities of real or fictional beings and objects. They will automatically lead you into a world that follows completely different rules from our own, and they will help your imagination to break free from conventions and accelerate into a fantastic new direction.

## The Mind-Matrix 2

This lists the qualities and abilities that are to be found in the mythical, comic-book or fictional heroes and superheroes of films and computer games. Of course, some of these are already being used in ads to woo target groups into buying particular products. The list will present you with a playground of ideas where you can leap around to your heart's content. It is important, however, that you should not allow yourself to hang onto visual clichés and things that are familiar to you. Try to feed your own curiosity and let your imagination create new scenes rather than old. On the other hand, you should not hamper yourself with unreasonable expectations, and although these key terms will spur you to new ideas, don't forget that sometimes the best solutions are simple and even banal. They may be right in front of your nose, but neither you nor anyone else has spotted them before.

The key terms in Mind Matrix 2 will open up wide fields of association, any one of which can set the creative spring bubbling. Choose one at random, and see where it leads you. It may also be productive if you apply the terms in Mind Matrix 2 to the categories of Mind Matrix 1.

# The Mind-Matrix I

### 1. Taking Images Apart
Divide images, scenes, objects into individual sections, play around with them in your mind's eye, and then put them together again, combining them with other things. Take the individual elements of scenes or objects, and develop a new idea for each of them.

### 2. Make Connections
Take separate items and combine them into something new. Connect up styles, picture elements, genres, media or scenes to create an original form. Replace some parts with new ones. Link together items that are as different as possible, that have never been put together before.

### 3. Make More Of Something
Enlarge certain areas, increase certain elements, exaggerate one detail. What could be added to or over-emphasized? What could be doubled, tripled, heightened, accumulated, piled up, inflated? What would a completely unnatural exaggeration look like?

### 4. Shrink It Down
Halve, shrink, reduce objects, scenes, features. Enter the microscopic realm and find out what the tiniest things can do, where you can put them, what insights they give you: cell division, splitting the atom, electrochemical processes inside the human brain.

### 5. Do The Opposite
Take a particular feature or scene, and turn it into its opposite. Twist familiar elements. facts, feelings, objects, behaviour, opinions; make old things new, and turn things upside down.

### 6. What Is Like This?
What is similar to the scene or the object you're looking for? What functions in a similar way, or follows the same principles? Find a suitable analogy or metaphor. Look for technical comparisons in nature, and for natural comparisons in technology.

### 7. Breaking The Laws Of Nature
What natural laws are there that have not yet been broken? What would be the consequences of breaking, changing, misusing or overturning the laws of electromagnetism or gravity? What new natural laws could be devised and applied to the real world?

### 8. Breaking The Rules
What are the rules and conventions associated with your project: social, sexual, sporting, behavioural, legal, visual? Which ones can be varied, broken, modified, reinterpreted, turned on their heads? Which rules could you break to provoke or shock people?

### 9. Seeing The Invisible
What is still invisible to the eye and to the other senses? What has never been seen before: emotions, musical notes, other sounds, magnetism, physical processes, death? What lies inside the human body: the heartbeat, detoxification of the liver, neural networks in the brain?

### 10. Make It Ambiguous
How can scenes be designed to be ambiguous, or staged in a manner that can be interpreted in different ways? How can pictures, scenes or characters take on multiple meanings or produce optical illusions? How can you use optical illusions or paradoxes to give objects or situations new meanings?

### 11. Putting Time In The Picture
Open different time windows simultaneously in a scene or medium. Go back into the past, travel through time, slow things down, speed things up. How can time influence or change images or scenes? What can you make visible by manipulating time?

### 12. Space and Perspective
From what angle has a scene never been shown or observed? What perspectives or camera angles contradict the laws of nature? What perspective is alien to the spectator's normal way of seeing? How would things look through the unfamiliar eyes of an animal, an object, an alien?

### 13. Shape and Colour
Can style and mood be manipulated by means of colour changes? What effect do space and form have on colour, and vice versa? Could you use forms that are not found in nature? What combinations of colours have never been tried?

### 14. Light and Shade
How can you strengthen the effect of light and shade? How could they become the central feature of a scene or object? What has never before been tried with light and shade? What can be added or left out? Can light and shade be manipulated or used in new ways?

# The mind-matrix 2

| | | |
|---|---|---|
| New forms of energy | Obscure languages | Willpower |
| Climbing skills | Control of cosmic forces | Awareness of objects |
| Extra limbs | Control of the laws of nature | Transfer of energy |
| Additional sensory organs | Empathy | Clairvoyance |
| Enhanced senses | Controlling fire | Talking to animals |
| Heat and flame resistance | Creating new natural laws | Sonar |
| Ability to fly | Hypnotic powers | Control of animals |
| Production & control of light | Creating illusions | Other dimensions |
| Weather control | Enhanced hearing | Voodoo |
| Force fields | Panoramic vision | White magic |
| Telekinesis | Molecular change | Transformations |
| Production of ice and fire | Gravity control | Mind travel |
| Invisibility | Control of magnetism | Communicating with plants |
| Invulnerability | Awareness of other lifeforms | Energy resources |
| Healing | Warning sensors | Magic shield |
| Jumping and flying | Energy sensors | Animal senses |
| Energy doubling | Brainwaves | ESP |
| Body transformation | Control of energy fields | Genetic technology |
| Mutation | Hallucinations | Psychokinesis |
| Morphing and shape-shifting | Neutralization | Dermo-optics |
| Paralyzing and freezing | Mental forcefield | Chameleon skin |
| Shrinking | Premonitions | Animal telepathy |
| Enlarging | Seeing the future | Cell division |
| Regeneration | Levitation | Wave/particle duality |
| Making waves | Telepathy | Nanotechnology |
| Doppelgangers | Teleportation | Quantum physics |
| Splitting | Time travel | Black holes |
| Breath control | Truth detection | Antimatter |
| Super speed | Ultraviolet vision | Gamma rays |
| Resistance to acid and poison | Switching between worlds | Parallel universes |
| Two-dimensionality | X-ray vision | Time loops |
| Walking in the air | Long-distance vision | Time machines |
| Animal powers | Microscopic vision | Fairies |
| Magnetism and repulsion | Thought blocking | Demigods |
| Energy control | Thought manipulation | Mythical creatures |
| Mind control | Changing molecular structure | Goblins |
| Control of emotions | Unlimited memory | |
| Imitation and adaptation | Radar sense | |

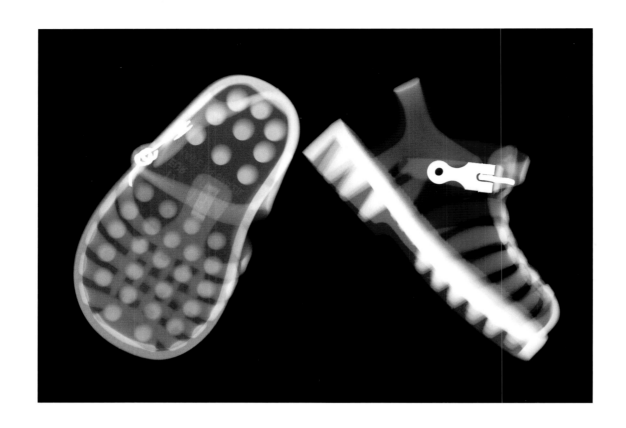

Above, right and opposite
**Photography:** Nick Veasey.
Radar Studio
www.nickveasey.com
www.untitled.co.uk

Below
**Client:** Levi Strauss & Co
**Agency:** Foote, Cone & Belding
**Creative Direction:** Brian Bacino
**Post-Production:** Rhinoceros
Visual Effects & Design
**Director:** Jim Sonzero
**Production:** Venus Entertainment
HSI Productions Inc.

### MAKING THE INVISIBLE VISIBLE

What surprising things would happen if you could see through things with X-ray vision? Would you be able to see the essence or 'soul' of objects? If you could make people or objects transparent, what would you see that has never been seen before: living things in living things, rays, fields of energy, chemical processes? Would you be able to see atoms vibrating, or the energy fields that hold materials together? How could you depict X-ray vision – how could this concept be made visible?

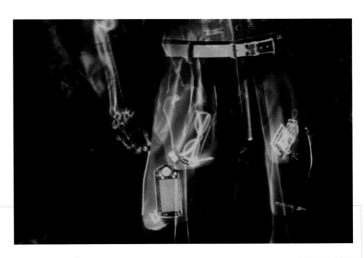

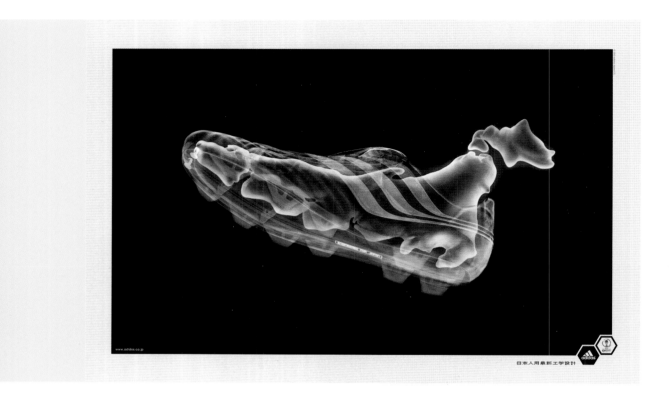

Left

Client: Adidas
Agency: Saatchi & Saatchi
Art Direction: Ikuo Toyama
Photography: Bryan Whitney
Illustration: Kensaku Nagao
Source: Lürzer's Archive 5/2002

   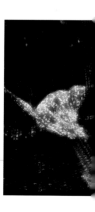

Right
**Client:** Dazed and Confused
**Designer:** Alex Rutterford
**Producer:** Christian Hogue
Lost In Space
www.lostinspace.com

Below
**Post-Production:** Ubik
www.ubik.it

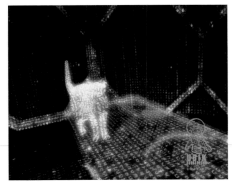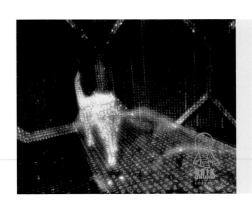

 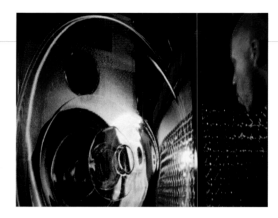 

## WAVES AND RAYS

What invisible physical or chemical processes can be depicted? How can you make processes visible that usually can't be seen? How can you portray waves, rays, or energy fields without having recourse to clichés? What do radiation, magnetism, shockwaves, radioactivity or energy fields consist of, and how do they affect us: smell, sound, taste, feelings? Can these phenomena be shown by way of their direct impact on objects or living creatures?

Above
Client: AKA Musik
Title: Euphoria
Producer: Steve Horton
Director: Marc Caro
Copyright by Premiere Heure

Below
Title: Soulkeeper (TV movie)
Post-Production: Blur
VFX Producer: Al Shier
VFX Supervisors: David Stinnett,
Steve Blackmon
Effects Animators: Neil Blevins
Tom Dillon, Kirby Miller, Bill Zahn

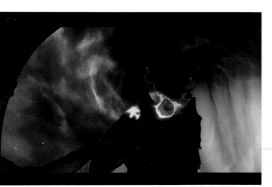
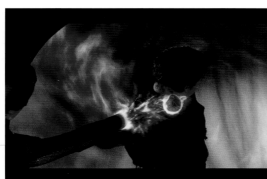

Above and below

**Computer Game:** Metroid Prime
**Publisher:** Nintendo
**Developer:** Retro Studios
© Nintendo of Europe GmbH
and used by permission.

In this scene we see the hero of the
computer game *Metroid Prime* using
the laser weapon in his arm.

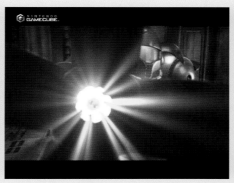

04      05      06      07

## ENERGY AND FORCEFIELDS 1

In what unusual ways could you depict the origin or impact of energy or light rays? How do the immediate surroundings react when a ray strikes them: shining, flashing, making a noise, changing colour? What might you find on the inside of the ray: sounds, images from the past, body parts, feelings, chemical processes? Take every element of these representations, and turn it into its opposite in order to uncover new aspects. Don't be afraid to make radical changes, and experiment with what may seem to be absurd forms of representation.

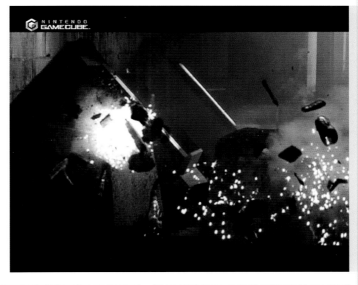

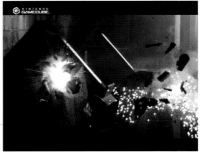

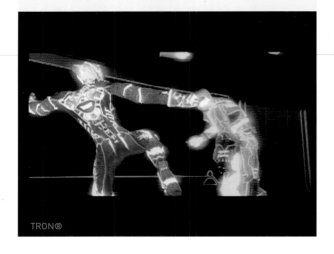

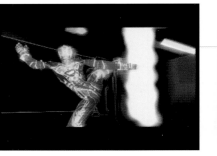

TRON®

## ENERGY AND FORCEFIELDS 2

How can you depict supernatural
powers, radiation or forcefields
without using clichés? How can you
visualize their shape and movement?
Borrow ideas from other spheres:
a whip, a jet of water, a chameleon's
tongue, a lasso, a snowball.

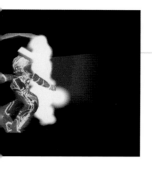 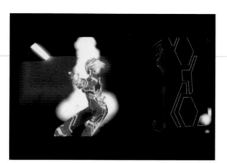 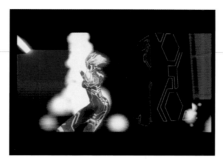 

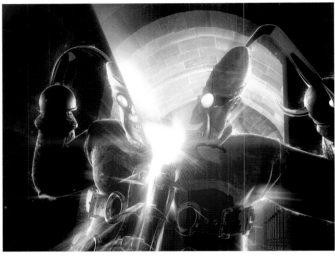

Left

**Title:** Gravités

**Project:** Short film

**Artists:** Thierry Bassement,
Frédéric Gesquière, Alexandre
Pérard

© Supinfocom / One Plus One

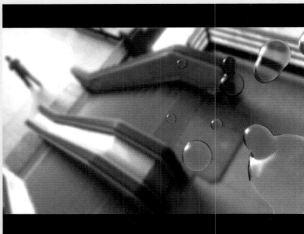

Below

In this BMW ad, a swimmer dives into a pool that has no water in it.
Client: BMW
Agency: Wight Collins Rutherford Scott Ltd
Creative Direction: Simon Robinson, Jo Moore
Director: Daniel Barber
Post-Production: Final Cut Ltd

BENDING THE LAWS OF NATURE 1

What are the laws of nature, and how can you circumvent or change them? How would your body and your lifestyle change if, for example, the force of gravity became stronger? What new factors would come into play if the Earth's magnetism were to increase? What natural laws could you manipulate in order to create new scenarios and images?

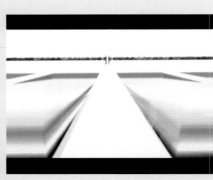

Client: Autotrader.com
Agency: Doner
Director: Buddy Cone
Creative Direction: Steve Fawcett
Production: Palomar Pictures
Post-Production: Digital Domain

Client: Levi Strauss & Co
Agency: Bartle Bogle Hegarty
Director: Jonathan Glazer
Special Effects: Framestore CFC
Creative Direction: Stephen Butler

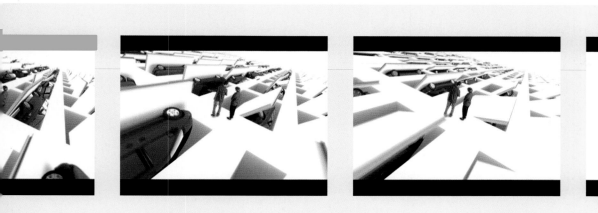

### BENDING THE LAWS OF NATURE 2

'What if...?' is the question that unlocks the door from reality into fantasy. What if people could breathe under water, what if gravity suddenly switched off, what if we could run up walls? Reverse the laws of life and nature, and find new ways of depicting fantastic and impossible worlds. It is important that you follow up your ideas and develop every aspect to its full potential. You will soon realize that all things are connected, and if you change a law of nature, it will have a domino effect on all areas of life.

Left and above
**Client:** Gaz de France
**Title:** Dolce Vita
**Agency:** Australie
**Director:** Bruno Aveillan
**Production:** Quad
**Post-Production:** La Maison
© Australie – Quad

Right

In the style of the film *Crouching Tiger, Hidden Dragon*, the heroine of this ad runs up a wall in order to escape from her pursuers.
Client: Visa International
Agency: BBDO/Guerrero Ortega
Art Direction: David Guerrero
Director: Bruce Hunt
Production: @radical.media
Post-Production:
Fin Design & Effects

Left
Photography: Scheffold.Vizner
Zürich/Switzerland
www.scheffold.vizner.com

Below and opposite
Client: Nokia
Title: Moving Mountains
Agency: Bates Singapore
Creative Direction: Petter Gulli
Art Direction: Roald Van Wyk
Director: David Deneed
Post-Production: Film Graphics

In this commercial you can see a man in the countryside sending a
picture to his girlfriend through his mobile. Just as he is sending it,
an army of workers arrives. They completely dismantle the landscape,
and rebuild it in his girlfriend's office. In this way, she can experience
the scene as if she were there on the spot.

## EVERYTHING IS POSSIBLE

If you want to show the usefulness of a product, you can exaggerate it to the highest degree. Come up with the formula, and then make it bigger, stronger, higher, longer, brighter, louder, tastier. There are no limits to the quest for effect, so what images and scenes can you create to take it to the max?

Left
Client: Nintendo
Title: Symphony
Agency: Leo Burnett
Director: Bruno Aveillan
Production: Quad
Post-Production: La Maison
© Leo Burnett – Quad

Right
Collage of 80 images
Photography: Scheffold.Vizner,
Zürich, Switzerland
www.scheffold.vizner.com

## SETTING THE IMAGE FREE

Whatever you are imagining, keep conscious control of the images. Think of something you have never seen before. Look around you, and transform your images into something new and different. How can you transform the world around you by imagining fantastic things happening right at this moment? Whatever you are working on, the key to great ideas is the ability to conjure up something unexpected.

Above
Client: BT Broadband
Agency: St Lukes
Creative Direction:
Julian Vizard, Al Young
Director: Garth Jennings
Special Effects: Chris Knight,
Dave Smith, Lorraine
McLaughlin, Neil Davies

Left
Artist: Placebo
Song: Slave to the Wage
Project: Music video, Virgin Music
Director: Howard Greenhalgh
Post-Production: Eye Animation

This scene is from the trailer for the computer game *Tom Clancy's Rainbow Six 3*™.
In the atrium of a tall building, a rocket is aimed directly at a helicopter that is
circling above the glass dome. On impact, the helicopter plunges through the
dome and down into the interior of the building, just missing some people.

Computer Game Trailer:
Tom Clancy's Rainbow Six 3™
Publisher: Ubi Soft Entertainment
Developer: Ubi Soft Entertainment

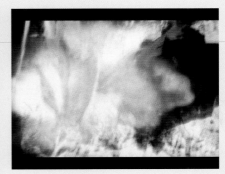

Above left
**Client:** Tank magazine
**Illustration:** Sarah Howell
**Artist Management:** Justice
www.cjustice.com

Below left
**Client:** Heelys
**Source:** Lürzer's Archive

*L/S STATEMENT FLEX TOP*
*FILAMENT TIGHT*

Client: Nike
Agency: Wieden&Kennedy
Art Direction: Merete Busk
Photography: Juan Algarin
Illustration: Sebastien Jarnot,
Perrine Dorin
Source: Lürzer's Archive 3/2002

Photography: Peter Keil
Digital Art: Ralf Eikenroth
www.keil-photography.com

IMAGES IN MOTION

What would be the most impressive
way of showing movement in stills or
photos? What forms of motion have
never been captured in pictures?
What camera angles could best
convey movement? How could you
show moving objects in an unusual
way or follow them while they are in
motion? What tracking shots would
be impossible? How have moving
objects never been shown before?

Above right
**Photography:** Ray Massey
www.raymassey.com

Below right
**Artist:** I Mother Earth
**Song:** Like The Sun
**Project:** Music video
**Compositor:** Steven Lewis
**Agency:** Oz Media
**Post-Production:** Spin Toronto

Client: Sécurité Routière
Agency: Lowe Alice
Art Direction: Laurent Chehere
Creative Direction: Celine Lescure
Photography: Laurent Seroussi

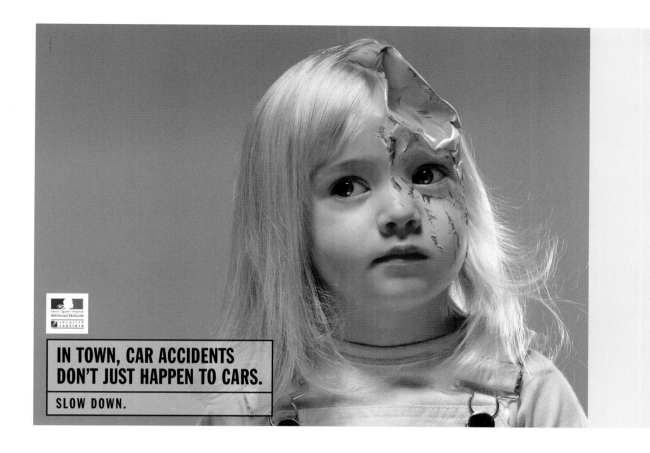

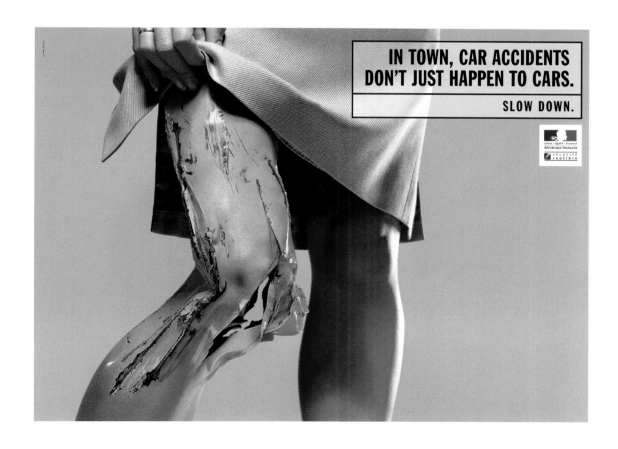

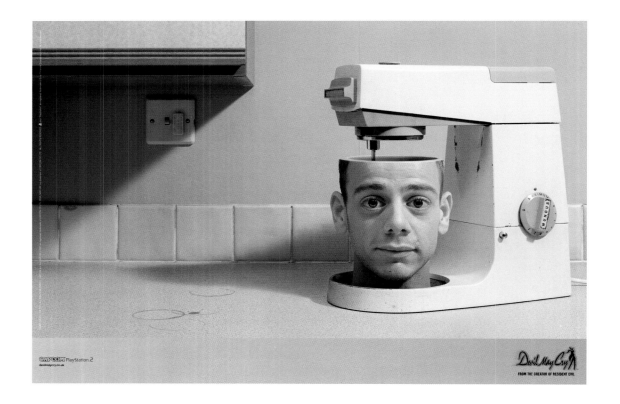

Above left
**Client:** Andersen Consulting
**Art Direction:** Tom Peck
**Digital Artist:** Michael Kerbow
**Photography:** David Langley

Below left
**Client:** Capcom Eurosoft Ltd
**Product:** Devil May Cry (computer game)
**Agency:** Banks Hoggins O'Shea FCB
**Art Direction:** Rob Fletcher
**Photography:** Malcolm Venville

Client: Sony Playstation
Agency: TBWA\Hunt\Lascaris
Art Direction: Gareth Lessing
Creative Direction: Frances Luckin,
Sandra de Witt
Photography: Clive Stewart
Digital Artist: Beith Digital

'Bring someone back to life.
Donate organs.'
Client:
Brazilian Surgeons Association
Agency: Giovanni FCB
Art Direction: Carlos André Eyer
Photography: Platinum

Left and below
Illustrations: David Ho
www.davidho.com

## BODY WORLDS

How many ways can you find
to change the bodies of people
or animals – linking them with
other elements, enlarging parts,
combining features from different
living things, leaving parts out,
putting parts in, giving them new or
additional functions, taking elements
from the animal kingdom, making
the invisible visible? What would
be surprising, unique, unheard of?
Depending on the project, there is
virtually no limit to the body worlds
you can create, or the imaginary
creatures you can bring to life.

Client: Megafestatie/Axion
Agency: Duval Guillaume
Art Direction: Philippe De Ceuster
Creative Direction:
Giullaume van der Stighelen
Photography: Philippe Claes

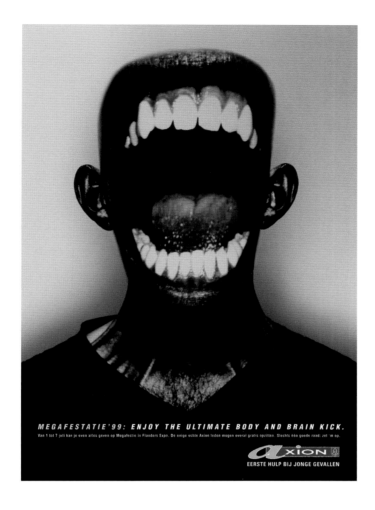

'If it were at your house, would
you complain?' Campaign against
sea pollution.
Client: Greenpeace
Agency: Giovanni, FCB
Art Direction: Carlos André Eyer
Creative Direction:
Adilson Xavier, Cristina Amorim
Photography: Leonardo Vilela

# 8. Styles, Trends and Genres

Today we live in a rich mixture of different cultures, styles, trends, genres, fashions and designs that often lead to completely original and surprising forms of visual expression. It has become quite normal for particular trends to transcend media boundaries and cross-fertilize games, advertising, music videos, films, the Internet and animation.

There is now an enormous demand for innovation, and creatives that confine themselves to the ideas and models of the last hundred years or so will soon find themselves trapped in a cul de sac. It is only a matter of time before new influences such as exotic cultures or ancient history begin to combine with current trends. What we are experiencing right now is probably only the beginning, for the combination of different elements that originally had no connection offers the greatest potential for the production of new visual ideas and styles. Here we have a basic strategy for creative invention: what things can be combined in order to produce something new? This area of our lab will show you just a small selection of the enormous range of styles, fashions and designs that are being used in computer games, commercials, posters, films and animations today.

Left and opposite, above
Client: Diesel Jeans
Agency: KesselsKramer
Art Direction: Krista Rozema
Photography: Carl-Johan Paulin
Source: Lürzer's Archive

Opposite, below
Client: Harvey Nichols
Agency: Mother
Photography: Johan Fowelin
Source: Lürzer's Archive

## NEW COMBINATIONS

Nowadays computer games like *Tomb Raider* are made into films, and films like *Star Wars* become computer games. What sort of things can be moved between genres? What genres can be combined, and what subjects can be linked to something new? Can you think of a film that employs the visual style of a computer game, or a stage play made into a computer game? Are there visual styles that are used in particular media but have never yet been tried in others? Which of these styles might be linked to something new, and which elements can be separated from existing styles to be used elsewhere?

The life of **HARVEY NICHOLS**

Client: Metz/Westbay
Agency: HHCL/Red Cell
Art Direction: Jonathan Burley
Post-Production: Glassworks Ltd
Director: Edna McCallion
Animation: Cako & Varga

This music video is completely
computer animated. Only the eyes
and mouth were added later.
Artist: Björk
Song: All Is Full Of Love
Project: Music video
Post-Production: Glassworks Ltd
Director: Chris Cunningham
Production: Black Dog Films

01    02    03

Left

Campaign for snow, surf and
skatewear label 55DSL
Client: 55DSL
Agency: KesselsKramer
Art Direction: Karen Heuter
Photography: Bart Oomes
Source: Lürzer's Archive

## PLAYING WITH STYLES 1

Take individual elements or typical characteristics of various styles and mix them to create something new: cultural or historical styles, current trends, styles used in particular media or branches. What architectural ideas are not fashionable at the moment? What fashions have not yet featured in product design? What advertising trends have not yet featured in computer games?

Above
Client: Cingular Wireless
Agency: BBDO Atlanta
Post-Production: Colorado FX
Director: Pat Solomon
Production: Fusion Films

Right
Ad for blackhead removal strips
Client: Pond's
Agency: Ogilvy & Mather
Creative Direction: Marco Colín
Art Direction: Raymundo Váldez, Javier Zapatero
Illustration: Alejandro Rodriguez

Client: Blue Source
Illustration: Leo Marcantonio
Executive Producer:
Christian Hogue
www.lostinspace.com

Fig 125

Fig 127

Illustration: Sarah Howell
Artist Management: Justice
www.cjustice.com

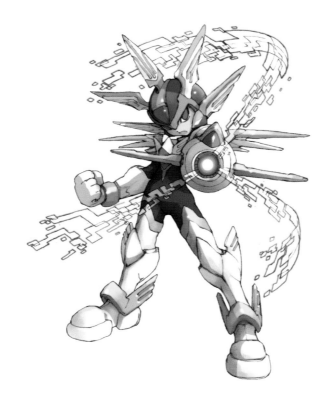

## ILLUSTRATION AND ANIMATION

Illustrations, animations, cartoons
and comic-book styles have such a
vast range of potential forms that
they can be used to fulfil almost any
function. Advertising in particular,
which sets such store by unique
identity, makes far too little use of
this visual language and its different
styles. What styles of animation and
illustration might be used in these
different media: films, games,
TV, mobile games, packaging,
computers, advertising?

Computer Game: Silent Hill 3
Publisher: Konami
Developer: KCET
© Konami Computer
Entertainment Tokyo
All Rights Reserved.

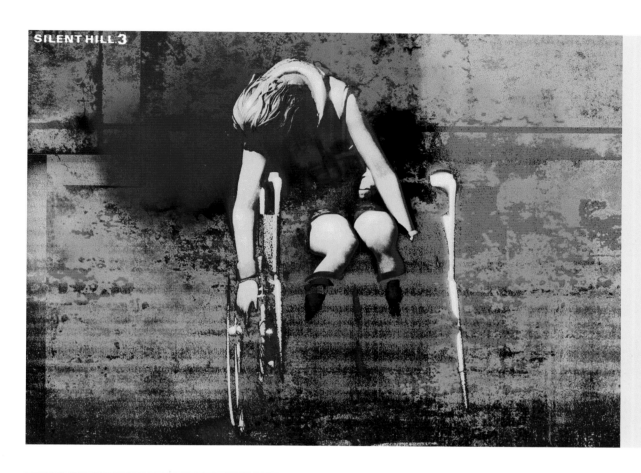

Client: Issey Miyake
Studio: Research Studios
www.researchstudios.com

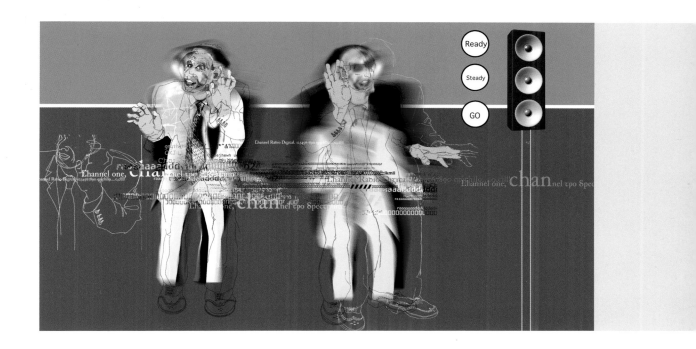

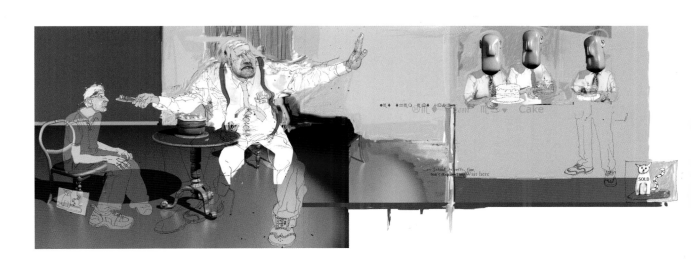

Illustration: Daniel Mackie

www.danielmackie.co.uk

Illustration: Phil Hale
melegrau@zoom.co.uk

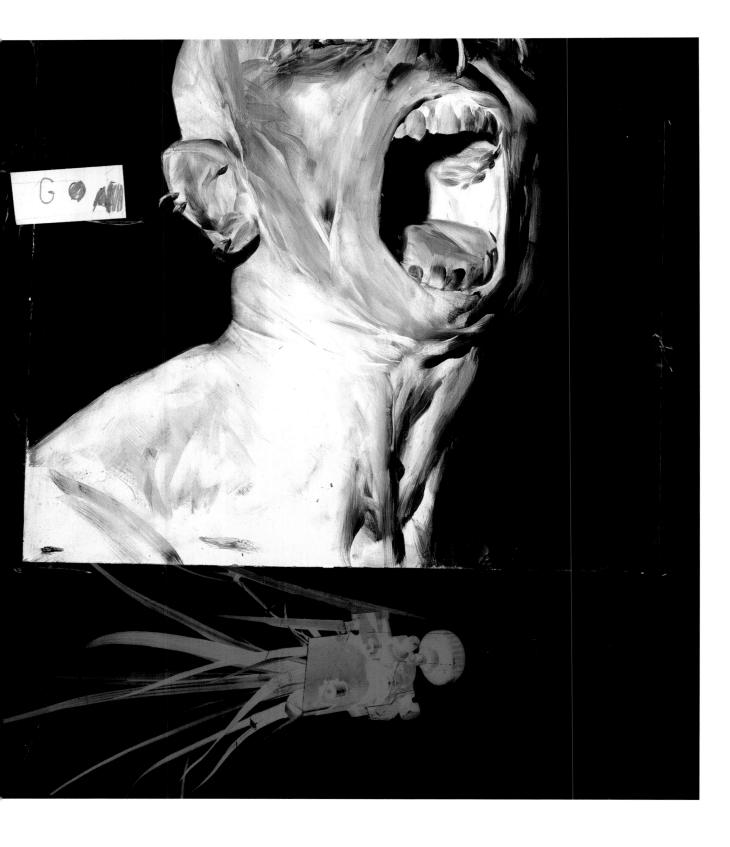

Illustration: Daimon J. Hall
Client: Powerhouse Productions
www.mantismedia.com.au

## PLAYING WITH STYLES 2

Take whatever you're working on at the moment, and imagine applying some of the following styles to it, paying careful attention to the changes that might occur: comic-books, cartoons, silent movies, stop-motion clay figures, flipbooks, illustrations, doodles, documents, collages, classical styles from the fine arts, exotic styles from foreign cultures.

**Title:** Tim Tom
**Project:** Short film
**Artist:** Cristel Pougeoise,
Romain Segaud
© Supinfocom / One Plus One

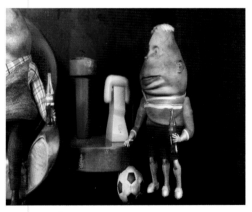

Client: Coca-Cola
Title: Super Sub
Project: TV ad
Agency: Wieden + Kennedy
Art Direction:
Jon Matthews, John Boyler
Post-Production: Duran
Director: Numero 6

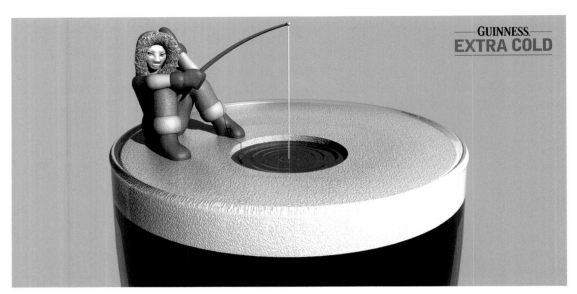

Above left
Client: Guinness Extra Cold
Agency: Abbott Mead Vickers BBDO
Art Direction: Jeremy Carr
Photography: Faiyaz Jafri
Source: Lürzer's Archive 1/2002


Below left
Computer Game: N.U.D.E.@
Natural Ultimate Digital Experiment
Publisher: Microsoft
Developer: RED Entertainment
© Microsoft Corporation.
All Rights Reserved.

N.U.D.E.@
Natural Ultimate Digital Experiment

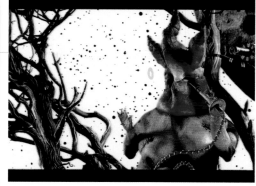

## PLAYING WITH STYLES 3

Illustrations, animations, comic and cartoon styles can be combined into new forms of expression. Which of these styles have never been put together? How could 2D animation be combined with 3D animation? How could old styles of illustration be integrated into new computer animation, and how could cartoons be combined with puppet animation using stop-motion techniques? Could such styles be integrated into realistic films? What visual style could be combined with animation to create something new?

Above right
**Title:** Ah Pook Is Here
**Project:** Short film
**Director:** Philip Hunt
**Producer:** Eddel Beck
**Post-Production:** Studio Aka
www.studioaka.co.uk

Below right
**Computer Game:**
Panzer Dragon Orta
**Publisher:** Sega
**Developer:** Smilebit Original Game
© Smilebit corporation /
SEGA CORPORATION

TRON®

 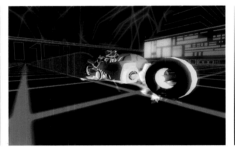 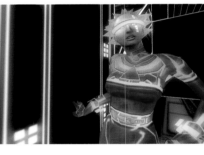

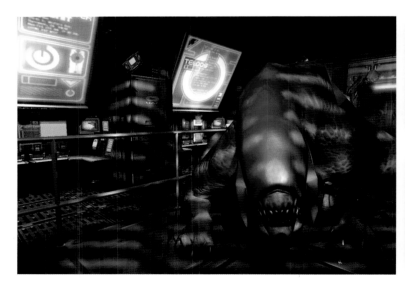 

Above left
**Computer Game:** Tron 2.0
**Publisher:** Buena Vista Games
**Developer:** Monolith
TRON® Owned by Cooper
Industries, Inc. and used by
permission. © Disney

Below left
**Computer Game:** Doom III
**Publisher:** Activision
**Developer:** id Software
© Activision, Inc.
All Rights Reserved.

**Title:** Delgo
**Project:** Animated film
**Production & Creation:**
Fathom Studios
©Electric Eye Entertainment
Corporation.
All Rights Reserved.

From Dream To Reality

# part 04

# Sketches, Layouts and Storyboards

{ **TEN-SECOND SUMMARY** Sketches, layouts and storyboards save time, money and nerves when it comes to the development of ideas, because they allow other people to see your ideas, and so prevent misunderstandings. Once an idea has been put down on paper, it generates a feedback loop in which the eye, the hand and the imagination can all stimulate one another.

There are nearly always three key qualities that enable exceptionally talented creatives to come up with success after success: the willingness to take risks, the quest for perfection, and the power of realization. In this context, willingness to take risks means the courage to try something unconventional, as for instance Walt Disney did in his pioneering work. The quest for perfection is the desire to reach a level that no one has ever reached before – enough is never enough, and a great idea is nothing compared to a stroke of genius. But the most essential of these three requisites is the will and the skill to turn ideas and imagination into reality so that other people can experience them. The first step towards this is often a quick sketch or a rough layout, which is why I am going to devote a few pages to this subject. For creatives in the worlds of advertising, animation and film, these doodles are the equivalent of the notes jotted down by composers, or the words and phrases scribbled by writers. Most creatives use doodles for three purposes: to record ideas for themselves, to show them to others, or to develop them in greater detail. In the earliest stages of idea-production, sketches are used all too rarely by people working in teams. If you want to get your colleagues to enthuse about your inspired idea, you will need to give it a visible form. At this stage, the quality of the drawing is relatively unimportant – a good concept will come across whatever the style – but it is a different matter when the germ of an idea has to be worked out in detail and the first layouts have to be designed. Sketches initially function like a feedback loop between imaginary images, drawing, and seeing. While the hand puts the image down on paper, the resulting picture may itself lead to new ideas. Of course it can happen that no matter how hard you try, you cannot actually conceive of something visually because you have quite simply never seen anything like it. In such circumstances it can be helpful to enlist reality as an aid to the imagination. It is said that the chief animator of Toy Story, Pete Docter, had difficulty finding an authentic way to depict a patrol of toy soldiers, and so he used a simple device. He wanted to show them on the march although their feet were permanently fixed to a plastic stand, and so he fastened a pair of shoes to a board and then started to walk in them. His colleagues studied his movements, and recorded them with sketches. This sort of thing is often a major problem for creatives, because they find that their drawings give an unsatisfactory representation of reality and of their ideas. Drawing is a talent that has to be learned and practised, and there are no special tricks or short cuts to make it easier.

## Characters and Environments

On the pages that follow, you will find several outstanding examples of sketches and designs from the fields of animation, scene design and computer games. I have tried to select pieces that show the development from sketch to end product, and you will see clearly that, at this world-class level, artistic talent is a prerequisite for presentation. We do not have space here to go into depth in every single field, which means that subjects such as conceptual art, cartoons, storyboards and production design are only touched upon briefly.

Client: Blockbuster Inc.
Agency: Doner
Art Direction:
Mark Cooke, Tom Gurisko
Production:
Complete Pandemonium
Animation: Tippett Studios
Sketches: Frank Petzold

### FROM DOODLE TO DESIGN

People at meetings often forget that ideas do not come into the world fully fledged, and so a doodle may well be their only chance of survival. Particularly when the brief is to produce something that has no precedent, and the sketch is the only visible evidence of birth, the step from doodle to design is absolutely crucial. You have probably seen for yourself how a skilfully executed concept will create far more enthusiasm from the team than a few uncertain strokes of the pencil.

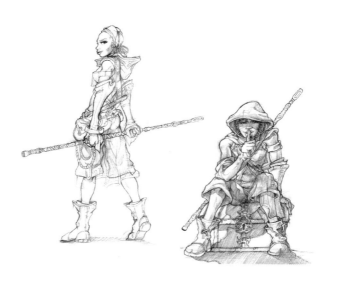

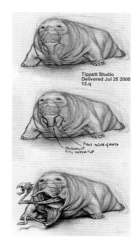

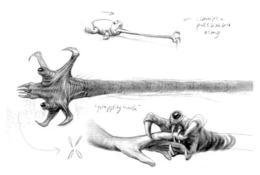

Above right
Project: 'Cutie Pie' Alien
Film Title: Evolution
Animation: Tippett Studios

Below right
Computer Game: P.N. 03
Character: Vanessa
Publisher: Capcom
Developer: Capcom ©CAPCOM
CO., Ltd. All Rights Reserved.

Artist: Péter Fendrik, Hungary
Title: Lady Bird

Computer Game:
FINAL FANTASY®X-2
Publisher: Electronic Arts
Developer: Square Enix Co., Ltd.
Main Character Design:
Tetsuya Nomura
Alternate Costume Design:
Tetsu Tsukamoto
© SQUARE ENIX CO., LTD.
All Rights Reserved.

Above and right
Computer Game:
Beyond Good & Evil
Publisher: Ubi Soft Entertainment
Developer: Ubi Soft Entertainment
© Ubi Soft Entertainment.
All Rights Reserved.

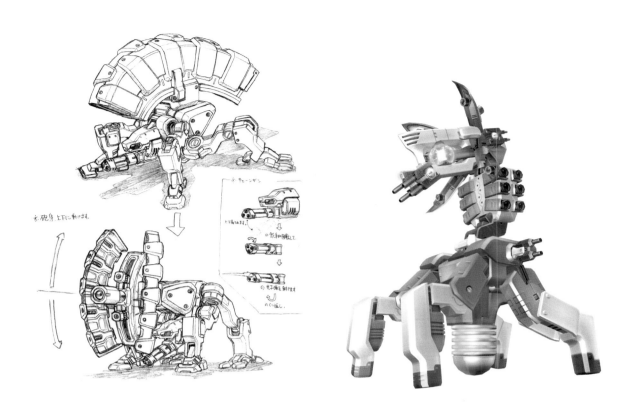

## SCENES AND STORYBOARDS

Alfred Hitchcock used to say that the storyboard was the real medium through which he realized his ideas. For this reason, he reckoned his work was already done before he started shooting, and indeed he often regarded the latter task as little more than a necessary evil. Steven Spielberg is another who plans his films beforehand down to the last detail, and he has every scene realistically depicted by conceptual artists. The storyboard is particularly important when it comes to staging special effects, as these scenes are generally far too complex to be captured by simple sketches or a few lines of description.

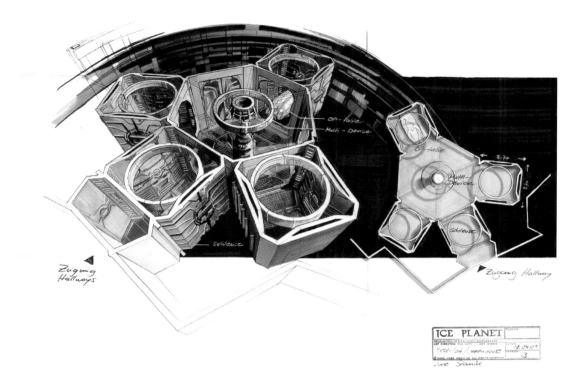

ICE PLANET

Above right
Title: Ice Planet
Work: Prop design
Production: H5B5 Media
Storyboard: Uwe Stanik

Below right
Title: The Commissioner
Production: Metropolis Film
Storyboard: Uwe Stanik

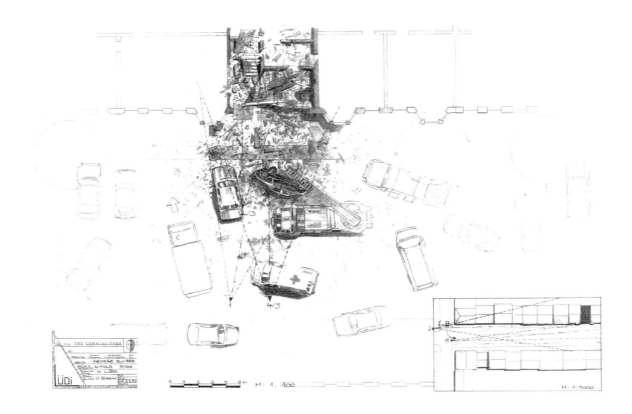

Title: The Commissioner
Production: Metropolis Film
Storyboard: Uwe Stanik

Title: Zweite Heimat
[student project]
Storyboard: Uwe Stanik

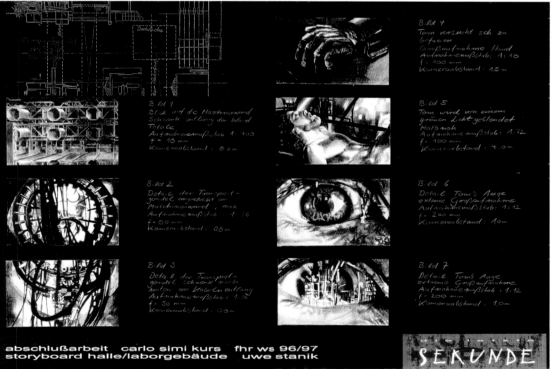

Above and right
Title: Die Letzte Sekunde
Production: Tiker Film
Storyboard: Uwe Stanik

part 05

Appendices